Modern Memory Quilts

A HANDBOOK *for* CAPTURING MEANINGFUL MOMENTS

12 PROJECTS + THE STORIES THAT INSPIRED THEM

Suzanne Paquette

stashBOOKS.
an imprint of C&T Publishing

PUBLISHER: Amy Marson

CREATIVE DIRECTOR: Gailen Runge

ACQUISITIONS EDITOR: Roxane Cerda

MANAGING EDITOR: Liz Aneloski

EDITOR: Katie Van Amburg

TECHNICAL EDITOR: Debbie Rodgers

COVER/BOOK DESIGNER: April Mostek

PRODUCTION COORDINATOR: Tim Manibusan

PRODUCTION EDITOR: Jennifer Warren

ILLUSTRATOR: Valyrie Gillum

PHOTO ASSISTANT: Mai Yong Vang

COVER PHOTOGRAPHY by Vivian Doan

STYLE AND EDITORIAL PHOTOGRAPHY by Vivian Doan; **INSTRUCTIONAL PHOTOGRAPHY** by Mai Yong Vang of C&T Publishing, Inc., unless otherwise noted

Library of Congress Cataloging-in-Publication Data

Names: Paquette, Suzanne, 1970- author.

Title: Modern memory quilts : a handbook for capturing meaningful moments - 12 projects + the stories that inspired them / Suzanne Paquette.

Description: Lafayette, CA : Stash Books, an imprint of C&T Publishing, Inc., 2019.

Identifiers: LCCN 2018015937 | ISBN 9781617455650 (soft cover)

Subjects: LCSH: Patchwork--Patterns. | Quilting--Patterns. | Commemorative quilts. | Clothing and dress--Remaking.

Classification: LCC TT835 .P35185 2019 | DDC 746.46/041--dc23

LC record available at https://lccn.loc.gov/2018015937

Printed in the USA

10 9 8 7 6 5 4 3 2 1

Dedication

For Michel and Luca, the two people on earth who bring the deepest emotion to my life and whose stories never grow old. I love you most.

Acknowledgments

A book cannot be created in a vacuum nor without support. My heartfelt thanks goes to:

Mom, Dad, and Matt, for your love and unwavering support, and to my mom, who started my life's path when she taught me to sew.

The Bocks, David, Heather, Jacqueline, Linda, Lucy, Marie-Jo, Maeve, Shanna and Ivo, Tiffany, Tinka, and the women of MEM: I am grateful for your support in my work and in my life. Thank you for making me laugh, cry, and persevere.

Vivian Doan, for her talent, dedication, friendship, and the amazing photographs in this book.

Amy Marson and Roxane Cerda, for their friendship and wisdom in publishing and life. Katie Van Amburg, Debbie Rodgers, April Mostek, and the C&T team for their talent and hard work— and for getting the big picture of what's truly important.

Aurifil, Camelot Fabrics, Fairfield Processing Corporation, Robert Kaufman Fabrics, and Soak Wash, for contributing materials for the projects and being great at what you do.

Cinzia Allocca, Stephanie Baldwin, Tom Bock, Kaleb Philips, Mitali Ruths, Marina Segalovitch, Debbie Soll, and Karyn Valino, for your talent and help with the quilts and photography. This book simply wouldn't have happened without you.

And last but not least, Tasha, Jacqueline, Vivian, Jeffrey, Clay, Linda, Brendan, Sonja, Diana, Sophie, the McClelland/Paquette/Sachowski family, Anna, Michel, Luca, Mitali, and Liz—your willingness to share your stories with me is a gift that has changed me forever. I only wish I had asked you to tell them sooner. Thank you.

Contents

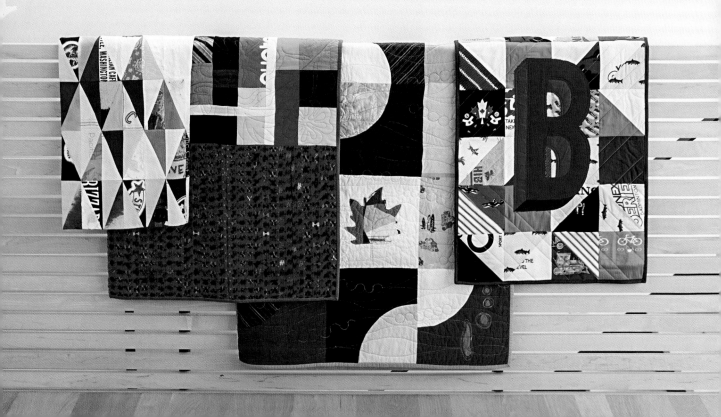

JOY

30

40
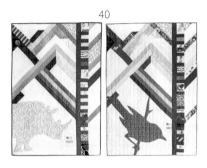

52

60
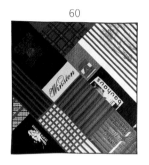

COMFORT

70

76

88

96

GENERATIONS

108
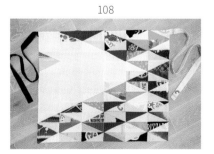

118

128
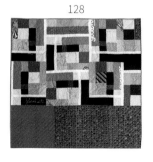

134

Introduction

This book contains modern heirloom quilts I designed and made for different families, each quilt inspired by their stories. When I sat down to interview each person for this book, I found that every story about the clothing chosen for the modern memory quilt had an unexpected depth. I knew the stories would be interesting, but I did not expect to be so intensely moved by each interview. The layered emotions behind what, on the surface, seemed like straightforward memories created complex and meaningful narratives—as unique as the people that told them. This should not be surprising: Each of us is a storyteller with something different to say and also something to learn. Yet I was struck by how I'd never had these conversations with these people in my life before—some of whom I'd known for a very long time. After that realization, the importance of telling these stories (in this book, but more importantly, in our own daily lives) became amplified for me.

Themes emerged from the stories in every situation: Some joy and happiness and some sadness, pain, or discomfort was expressed. In some cases, joy was hard-won or heightened by challenges and the difficult feelings that come with going through an emotional trial. In others, pain and sadness were countered by sweet, fond memories and happy times that were a balm to broken or homesick hearts. There was always a mix of emotions—whether for a typically "happy" memory, like the birth of a child, or for a "sad" memory, like the death of a loved one. That nuanced complexity, I think, is precisely the reason that the people and memories represented in memory quilts are so important to us.

Creating quilts made with fabric that is woven with memories and emotion is meaningful and rewarding work. The projects in this book celebrate or commemorate different life events. Use them as a springboard for a quilt that is personal and suited to the recipient—regardless of the original use in this book. For each project, I've indicated technical advice on which fabrics are best suited to the design.

I hope that you find inspiration in these pages—not only for quilts but also to tell your own stories (or those of someone else) with needle and thread.

Memory Keeping

When I worked for *Cirque du Soleil*, our internal newsletter included letters from spectators who had written in about how their evening enchanted them. At times they were moved to tears by the weight of the moment but also uplifted by the personal connection they felt.

Creating modern memory quilts is, for me, a similar experience: taking quiet connections and complex emotions—a combination of funny, sad, wondrous, thought-provoking, or everyday memories—and pulling them down to earth just enough to convert them into something tangible.

A talisman of sorts, the quilt helps bring your most personal reflections about a person, time, place, or event (and sometimes all of those) to the forefront— a chance to reconnect with who and what is most important.

Remembering

When working on a personal project, I look at photos, journal entries, and other physical keepsakes to remember and look for recurring patterns in the details. Listening to music or someone's voice, or experiencing the feel and smell of their clothing, can also be powerful reminders.

Specific pieces of clothing might conjure up particular memories and give inspiration for the quilt's theme. I always start with how something or someone makes me feel and then figure out how to put those feelings in quilt form through shape, color, layout, movement, and texture.

With Michel + Luca's Papa and Son Quilt (page 134), I wanted to create a quilt that celebrated both the joy of becoming a father and the unique bond Michel has with our son by combining their clothing. I also wanted to stop time for just a moment. Every time our son grows and changes, it's bittersweet—I miss his smaller, younger self yet love who he is becoming. Having pieces of his baby clothing in the quilt offers an instant connection to those wonderful, fleeting days (and sleepless nights).

Photo by Suzanne Pâquette

Michel + baby Luca

Michel + Luca now

Take time to explore the emotions and memories associated with the quilt you are about to make. In the end, you will have a living keepsake. You will pass memories from generation to generation through the storytelling of your personal quilt.

Documenting

The first time I made a modern heirloom memory quilt, it was from my son's baby clothes. I will never forget the first cut of my shears into the tiny onesie. Instead of "measure twice, cut once," it was more like "measure twenty times, hold your breath, cut, and hope for the best!"

It gets easier with each piece of clothing (see Emotions + Cutting, at right)—and it's almost always easier with someone else's clothing. I've also come to believe that even a "wrong" cut can be turned into a "right" cut. If things don't go according to plan, you will figure it out. Sometimes you end up with something even better than you imagined.

EMOTIONS + CUTTING

Nothing reveals your true emotions like preparing to cut into a piece of clothing that has a strong memory attached to it. If you really resist, put the item away for another day, week, or month. When you are ready, you will use it—or choose to keep it intact.

PHOTOGRAPHING CLOTHING

It's never a bad idea to photograph clothing before you cut it up—especially the outfit your kid wore home from the hospital. Or your wedding dress. Or your mother's favorite shirt. Preserving meaningful clothing through photos is a great way to hold on to the memories without taking up closet space.

For every memory quilt I make, I photograph all the clothing. Whether the photographs make their way into albums or scrapbooks or just sit quietly on a hard drive, I've found that people (including myself) like to have the original pieces documented just in case.

You can go as simple or complex as you like. I often photograph it fairly simply, using a white background and hanging the garment on a nice hanger, lying it flat, or washi taping it to the wall.

Children's Clothes

Adding props

Simple white background

Try laying items on interesting backgrounds.

Don't forget close-ups of details!

Using negative space highlights the size of the baby clothes.

Photos by Suzanne Paquette

Adult Clothes

Focusing on sections of a larger piece of clothing can make a more dynamic photo.

Photos by Suzanne Paquette

Movement created by the wind or a fan helps clothing on hangers have more life.

Fold hard-to-photograph items.

Perspective

Because memory quiltmaking is emotional by nature, timing and perspective are key when selecting clothing.

I have found that most people are not ready to part with the clothing of a loved one who has passed until at least a few years after their death. Grief, of course, is a very personal experience, devoid of a linear path. We each need time to process loss in our own way.

When a friend or family member has lost someone, I gently remind them to keep their loved one's clothing, or at least their favorite pieces, if there is any possibility that they might want a quilt made. Even a few pieces can make a meaningful quilt.

People are often upset after giving their children's sentimental clothes away. It's never too late to start saving. If the baby clothing is gone, start saving toddler clothing or school-age, teenager, or adult clothing. One day, those clothes will be just as filled with memories as the baby clothes.

At the end of each season, I separate clothes that no longer fit my son into quilt, donate, and toss piles. This keeps things manageable and ensures that the pieces I won't use in a quilt aren't cluttering up our storage. Less frequently, our adult clothes that are worn out or that we are tired of get sorted into the same piles.

Sometimes after keeping clothing for a season or two, my perspective on it changes. If I can't remember why I hung on to something and I don't particularly like it, I usually remove it from the stash. Like fabric, there rarely seems to be a problem of "too little clothing" when you regularly collect it.

Empathy + Design

Soon after I started making memory quilts for other people, it became clear that understanding the story and feelings behind the quilt was paramount in guiding the design process. It wasn't about me and my creative vision—it was about the person who would love and use the quilt.

When I meet a client or friend for a new commission, I go through the clothing with them and ask them to tell me about the pieces and the associated person or event. A new story emerges that guides the quilt design.

In the interviews for this book, I asked the same series of questions to each person. Every single person had an underlying theme to his or her answers. This helped me make design decisions for each quilt.

If you are making a quilt for someone and would like to have a conversation with them, try asking them the questions from the memory quiltmaking interview (at right).

If you are making a memory quilt for yourself, I still encourage you to answer the interview questions. An underlying theme may emerge—one that you maybe hadn't realized was there.

FINDING *your* COLLABORATIVE VOICE

If you are making a memory quilt for someone else, collaboration is key.

Like many creative people, I suffer from *imposter syndrome*, the fear of being exposed as a fraud. When this fear takes up too much room, I become insular, fearful of exposing the gaps in my knowledge, and afraid of letting in the ideas of others; I become greatly diminished in discovering new possibilities and letting the work (and myself) evolve. With tough love and hard work, I'm able to be open to the ideas of others while staying true to who I am creatively. I often have a vision of a project's creative direction, but collaborating with the eventual owner of the quilt is worth the time and effort. It always makes me a better designer.

MEMORY QUILTMAKING INTERVIEW

1. Whose clothing will be used to make this quilt? What is your favorite memory of them? What do you most admire about them?

2. What are a few of your favorite pieces of clothing that you chose for the quilt? Are there any specific memories or feelings that you associate with these pieces?

3. Why do you want to have a quilt with your loved one's clothing made?

4. What feels like love to you? What does the love of this person/people feel like to you?

5. What story do you want your kids, grandkids, friends, or future generations to know about the clothing in this quilt, who it belonged to, and your relationship to them?

Empathy is at the heart of design.
Without the understanding
of what others see, feel, and experience,
design is a pointless task.
—Tim Brown, IDEO

Materials First

When I was studying fashion design, my professor's mantra was "Start with the fabric." It took me a bit of time to take this to heart; I preferred to start designing with cut, color, theme, and pattern.

There could not be more sage advice for making a memory quilt. The surface design, fabrication, color, and material of each piece of clothing impact the design and technical choices. The size of the graphic prints on the T-shirts guides the quilt or block pattern choice. Pocket and seam details may provide inspiration for placement and aid in the technical decision to eliminate or incorporate those details. Chunky knit sweaters, fur, or other bulky fabrics could be successfully included in a quilt design, but size and seams need to be taken into consideration.

Photo by Suzanne Paquette

Including garment details within block pieces

Un-fussy cutting

Photo by Suzanne Paquette

Fussy and "Un-Fussy" Cutting

I'm always looking for ways to reinterpret or give a modern twist to the idea of a memory quilt—especially those made with T-shirts. Fussy cutting plays a key role when making a quilt from clothing. When it's right for the quilt, I'll fussy cut around a detail in the clothing, centering the detail within the piece.

Often, though—especially with T-shirt text and other screen-printed designs—I "un-fussy" cut. This means slicing right through the printed design, rotating the angle, showing only part of a word, or playing on negative space by having only part of the print appear, creating an additional design element or point of interest.

If you are able to muster up the courage, try cutting your printed T-shirts and clothing improv style. Don't plan it—just place your ruler or template and cut. When I make a quilt for someone else, I ask them if they are okay with this. Sometimes it is not preferred.

Keep in mind that sometimes a less-than-ideal or unappealing placement will happen. If you are okay with taking that risk, forge ahead and see what happens.

Test-Driving Versus Improvisation

The best and worst thing about working with clothing is that there is only one of each piece. On one hand, each piece is as unique as the person that owned it; on the other hand, you can't buy another if you make an irreversible mistake. Once you start to cut, you can't go back. This is why I photograph the clothing (page 11) before cutting it.

If the design offers flexibility in placement (like *Ombré Hexies*, page 54) and I'm comfortable with the palette and selection, I have carte blanche from my client, or it's a personal quilt, I am more likely to improvise, cutting and building on my design wall.

Remember that mistakes can provide opportunity—ultimately, you may end up cherishing what seems undesirable at the time.

Tip: Coloring Sheets

If having a visual guide is helpful for you, download the free coloring sheets from my website (ateliersixdesign.com/downloads) to map out your color and clothing placement.

Color Stories

Color Basics + Color Comfort Zones

In memory quilting, it's important to let the clothing drive the color choices. This sometimes means working outside your color comfort zone—a great way to build color skills and challenge yourself!

Paying attention to how colors relate to each other is essential. You may choose a color direction, but once you start looking at the interaction of the colors, you may decide to go down a completely different path.

Sometimes your favorite clothing pieces won't work with the color scheme. Play with the color palette until you find a unifying element. (Try white, gray, or black if you have many pieces that don't go together color-wise.)

To bring together seemingly mismatched clothing, try arranging the clothing in different ways to see how the colors work together. Grouping colors together or creating gradations or ombrés can be effective. Playing around with color proportions can help a palette emerge: Having a lot of navy clothing does not mean you need to make a navy quilt—it could be orange with navy highlights.

Removing a piece from the mix can often help you see it in a new light and bring it back into the palette in a different way. I try not to remove important clothing pieces permanently, especially in a quilt for someone else, but sometimes one piece really can prevent a good quilt from being great. You can always work that piece into the quilt back.

If, after playing around with the colors, I still don't have a palette I love, I turn to Pinterest for an image that contains my colors or leads me to colors I could add to make my palette cohesive. Having a reference image provides a guide to check in with until the path becomes clear.

Photo by Dmirty Fisenko

This photo inspired me for Lois's Kindred Pillows, 8 Variations (page 96) that I made with my grandmother's fur coat. Pink was her favorite color, and I needed a bit of help getting out of my color comfort zone.

Give yourself time to play and experiment—before you know it, you'll have a harmonious composition.

Memory Quilt Construction

Tools

In addition to the usual assortment of quilting tools, there are a few specific tools I like to have on hand when making a quilt with clothing.

FABRIC SHEARS: These are the best tools for cutting clothing to prepare it for sewing.

PRESSING CLOTH: A pressing cloth is essential for starching fabric and protecting delicate or printed fabrics (like T-shirts).

TEMPLATE MATERIAL: If you are not cutting shapes that can be made with quilting rulers, it's helpful to have some transparent template material on hand. It allows you to easily cut a template and place it on clothing to fussy cut any details. I like to use Visi-GRID Quilter's Template Sheets (by C&T Publishing).

FUSIBLE AND NONFUSIBLE INTERFACING: Interfacing is helpful in stabilizing clothing fabric. My favorite fusible interfacing is Stabili-TEE Fusible Interfacing (by C&T Publishing).

NONPERMANENT MARKING TOOL: I use my Hera Marker for everything from quilting lines to cutting lines for half-square triangles and notch marks.

STARCH IN A SPRAY BOTTLE: Starching (page 24) is my preferred method of stabilizing stretchy fabrics. When I start a new memory quilt, I mix up a fresh batch of homemade starch (see Starch Recipe, page 25).

SHALLOW TUB FOR STARCHING: Working in a shallow tub allows me to starch each piece as I go. The sides of the tub help contain the starch, and I wash out the excess starch with a sponge when it builds up in the bottom of the tub. My favorite tubs are the Small Shallow Gorilla Tubs.

Preparing Clothing for Quilting

Memory quiltmaking with clothing that is not 100% woven cotton is much easier when you take some key steps to prepare and manage the fabrics.

NOTE | Clothing Quantities

Clothing quantities for all projects in this book are approximate. You may need more or less depending on the usable area of the garment you are using, fussy cutting, and your desired placement. If you do not have enough clothing, you can always substitute in some quilting cotton in the desired color.

PREWASHING

Prewashing clothing is not quite the same as prewashing quilting cotton. In my experience, clothing has a much wider range of outcomes for color bleed and other factors than quilting cotton.

If the quilt will be washed, I suggest washing at least a piece of each garment before you use it to test for colorfastness. Extra dye can often successfully be leached enough from clothing that it will not affect the quilt. And if it can't, you can opt to leave it out.

The upside is that some clothing, like baby clothing, has been washed and dried so many times that any change that was going to happen to the fabric has already occurred.

CLOTHING PREP

For the projects in this book, prepare the clothing as follows:

1. *Optional:* Photograph the clothing (page 11). Download a coloring sheet (page 16) and map out your color and clothing placement.

2. Prewash and dry the clothing (see Prewashing, at left).

3. Cut the clothing into flat pieces (see Cutting Clothing, next page). Cut off any seams unless they are desired for the quilt. For example, you may want to keep the bottom hem of a T-shirt.

4. Refer to Controlling Stretch (page 24) to stabilize the clothing pieces using starch, interfacing, or another method of your choice.

CUTTING CLOTHING

When I cut up a piece of clothing to prepare it for stabilizing, I generally cut along the seams as close as possible with a pair of fabric shears. For a shirt or one-sie, I cut both sides up the side seams and through the under-arm / inside arm. I then cut the shirt into smaller and/or flatter pieces, if necessary. Leaving the pieces as large as possible offers more cutting possibilities.

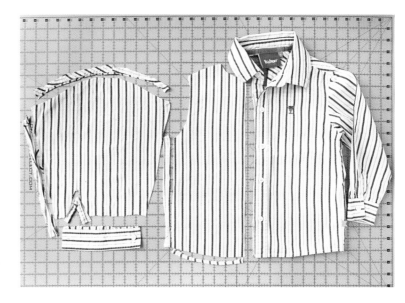

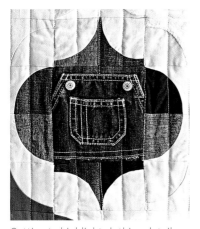

Cutting to highlight clothing details

Be mindful of any details you want to preserve, and make sure not to cut too close to them until you are sure if and how you want to treat them. In addition to pockets and plackets, shoulders and yokes can often have interesting details.

Tip: Plan Your Cutting

To maximize the use of each clothing piece and avoid cutting into usable space with a rotary cutter, plan your cutting.

If there are key features that you want to highlight from a piece of clothing, cut those pieces first. If you don't have a big enough piece of clothing fabric left to cut a particular pattern piece, you can always sew together two smaller clothing pieces to get the size you need.

Tip: Design Wall

Putting the pieces up on a design wall helps visualize how the design is coming together. It also allows you to make adjustments in how you cut the clothing as you go to achieve a pleasing result.

Tip: Highlight Flaws!

You don't always have to cut around stains or flaws in the clothing. Sometimes I highlight them with embroidery (like the ice cream stain on my son's T-shirt) or do some reverse appliqué with holes in clothing. Think of it as an opportunity to work in a bit of visible mending and character.

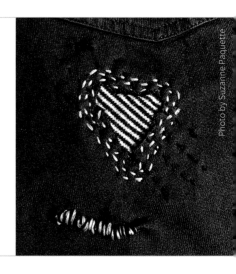

CONTROLLING STRETCH

One of the biggest challenges in working with clothing is controlling stretch—especially for items like T-shirts.

Starching

Starching clothing is easy and inexpensive, and it produces quilts that are supple and very similar to quilts constructed solely of quilting cotton. It takes a little longer to prep clothing with starch, but it is still my preferred way to stabilize most stretchy clothing fabrics. Starching is a temporary stabilizing solution that facilitates sewing but washes away when you wash the quilt.

You can follow one of two methods.

METHOD A: SPRAY STARCHING

1. Mix up a starching solution (see Starch Recipe, next page). Pour the cooled starching solution into a spray bottle.

2. Place the clothing piece right side up in a shallow tub.

3. Spray the piece evenly until starch covers the entire piece. It should be wet but not sopping.

4. Carefully lay the starched piece face side (starch side) down on an ironing board, covered with a pressing cloth.

5. Straighten the piece so that it is on grain and wrinkle free.

6. Place another pressing cloth on top of the starched clothing piece and press—with no steam—in an up-and-down motion. Be sure not to glide the iron along the piece while it is still wet. Continue pressing in this manner until the piece is mostly dry.

7. Carefully pull the piece from the ironing board. (It may stick a little, but that is okay.)

8. Flip the piece over, place the pressing cloth on top, and press the back side until it is flat and mostly dry.

9. Continue flipping the piece and pressing until it is fully dry. As the piece dries, it will not stick to the ironing board.

METHOD B: DIP STARCHING

When the weather is good and I am working with larger adult clothing, I prefer to dip starch. It is faster than spray starching.

1. Make triple or quadruple the amount of the starching solution in Starch Recipe (next page). Pour it into a shallow tub.

2. Dip the clothing pieces in one at a time. Ensure they are fully coated with starch.

3. Gently squeeze extra starch out of the piece.

4. Pin the piece to a clothesline or drying rack, making sure to hang it in a way that encourages even, flat drying.

5. The dip-starched pieces will drip a bit, so place a ground cloth underneath the drying area if necessary.

Shallow tub and
spray bottle for starching

MODERN MEMORY QUILTS

STARCHING TIPS + TRICKS

- Always use a pressing cloth both on the ironing board and on top of the fabric.

- Don't worry about white starch residue on pieces after they are pressed. It is just a concentration of dried starch, and it will wash out.

- Be careful not to burn the fabric when pressing starched pieces. Holding the iron too long in one position can burn the fabric. Be especially careful with white or light-colored clothing.

- Some people have found that starched garments attract bugs over time. While I have never experienced this, it is a good idea to plan on working through the starched quilt sooner rather than later or to use a different method to stabilize.

STARCH RECIPE

Ingredients

CORNSTARCH: 2–4 tablespoons

LUKEWARM WATER: ¼ cup

BOILING WATER: 2 cups

COLD WATER: 2 cups

ESSENTIAL OIL: 2–3 drops (*optional*)

Instructions

1. Whisk the cornstarch with the lukewarm water.

2. Add the boiling water and mix well.

3. Mix in the cold water and, if desired, the essential oil.

4. Pour into a spray bottle.

5. Shake before using.

Starch should be kept in the refrigerator in between quilting sessions. It will last 1–4 weeks refrigerated.

Fusible Interfacing

Applying fusible interfacing is quicker than starching, and it provides permanent stabilization to fabric, even after washing. I prefer Stabili-TEE Fusible Interfacing (by C&T Publishing) because it's lightweight and doesn't add a lot of bulk or stiffness to the quilt. The downside is that it is not 100% cotton. This may not matter if the fabrics are of a variety of fibers, but if I am making a cotton quilt, I prefer to have all-natural materials in the quilt.

Nonfusible Interfacing

Another option for stabilizing is using a lightweight piece of cotton or nonfusible interfacing as a stabilizing fabric. This permanent solution adds control but not stiffness. Unlike with nonwoven fusible interfacing, you can keep your quilt 100% cotton. I use this method to give heft to sheer fabrics or when I want to highlight, rather than hide, a hole in a piece of clothing.

To use this method, cut a piece slightly larger than the piece you want to stabilize; then baste together the two pieces. After basting, grade the seams so they differ by ⅛″ around the perimeter, which helps reduce bulk once you start piecing.

Sewing with Clothing

MANAGING BULK *in* SEAM ALLOWANCES

When working with fabrics of different weights, managing the bulk in the seams is important. You want to reduce the variance of bulk as much as possible between pieces, both for aesthetic appeal (to avoid having bumps when the fabrics get thicker) and technical reasons (quilting through dense or too-thick seam allowances can result in skipped stitches). There are a few tricks to managing bulk.

Pressing

Most instructions in this book advise you to press the seam allowances open. However, the behavior of your fabrics always trumps any pressing guidelines or preferences for seam allowances. This may mean pressing open, pressing to one side, nesting the seams, pressing to the dark side, or a combination of techniques.

I generally allow heavier-weight fabrics to lie flat, and I press the seam allowances toward the adjacent pieces (usually quilting cotton). Otherwise, I go with what the fabric is telling me. I usually choose whichever technique allows me to get the most even transition from one piece to the next.

NOTE | Pressing Cloths

When pressing starched fabric or screen-printed T-shirt graphics, use a pressing cloth. (Any scrap of light-colored cotton or muslin will do.) This prevents the fabric from burning and the screen-printing ink from melting or transferring to other parts of the quilt.

Keep the seams of heavyweight fabrics as flat as possible.

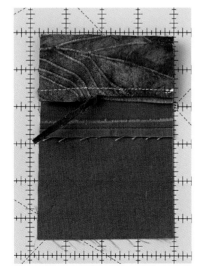

Grading

When being mindful of the pressing direction of the seam allowances is not enough, you may consider grading them. *Grading* is when one seam allowance is made smaller than the other (for example, ¼˝ and ⅜˝). Grading can be done for seams that are pressed to one side, but it has no effect for two seams pressed open.

To achieve this, cut the seam allowances a bit wider (⅜˝ or ½˝) than the standard ¼˝ seam allowance used in quilting. After cutting and sewing two pieces together with the larger seam allowance, trim the seam allowance of the fabric that lies closest to the batting by about ⅛˝. This staggers the seam allowances and makes a smoother transition from the seam to the edge of the seam allowance.

Hammering

If pressing and grading are not enough to get the seams to lie flat (enough), you can hammer them. This is a technique used in the construction of leather goods, and I borrowed it often when making hats from thick upholstery fabrics.

To hammer seams, place a scrap of fabric over the top of the seam and gently pound it a few times with a rubber mallet. This technique is particularly helpful for seams you may be worried about quilting through because it reduces the bulk.

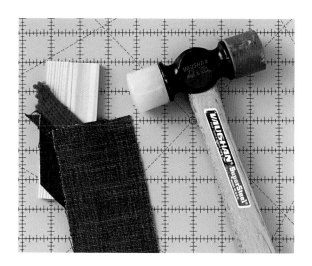

Tips and Tricks for Different Fabrics

LEATHER + SUEDE

Always use a pressing cloth when pressing blocks that contain leather or suede. A dry iron is preferred because steam dries these fabrics out.

Consider keeping these pieces small so you can quilt *around* instead of *through* them.

Use a walking foot when constructing blocks with these materials. It helps keep the fabric moving rather than sticking to the base of your machine.

KNIT SWEATERS

Before cutting through a knit sweater, consider how you will stabilize it. Generally, I have had success in cutting out a piece of knit sweater and carefully basting it to a piece of nonfusible cotton interfacing before piecing it into the quilt.

For a wool sweater, another option is to felt a piece of the sweater first, which keeps the fibers woven together.

As with leather and suede, a walking foot is helpful when working with knit garment pieces.

SHEER FABRICS

To incorporate sheer fabrics into a quilt, baste a piece of sheer fabric to a quilting cotton back (with a color chosen to complement the sheer), which acts as nonfusible interfacing.

SCREEN-PRINTED T-SHIRTS

Beware of screen-printed T-shirts printed with *plastisol*—the screen-printing ink that is rubbery in feel and sits well on top of the fabric. (Water-based inks and discharge screen prints sink into the fabric more and leave a softer hand.)

It is not always easy to quilt through plastisol-printed T-shirts because the needle doesn't easily move in and out through the rubbery, raised texture. If you absolutely want to use a print like this, plan on using smaller pieces that you can quilt around or test a scrap first.

Quilting + Finishing Tips

DENSITY *of* QUILTING

For quilts made with T-shirts or other stretchy fabrics that are starched—not fused with interfacing—I usually do a slightly denser quilting design. This helps keep the T-shirt pieces in place and prevents them from "bagging out" over time.

WORKING AROUND DETAILS

When considering your chosen quilting design, take into account all the little details—such as pockets, buttons, and ruffles—you have worked into the quilt. You may want to stitch around, not through, pockets (which serve as a great receptacle for little love notes). You can stitch around buttons or remove them for quilting and sew them back on afterward.

Before quilting, I find it helpful to place a piece of painter's tape over the item to avoid. That makes it easier to see it coming while you are quilting.

BINDING

The yardage for projects with binding has been calculated using a strip size of 2½″ wide for double-fold binding that finishes ⅜″ wide. If the edges of the quilt contain bulky fabrics, you may want to consider adding a bit of extra width to the binding strips to accommodate the extra bulk. Usually an extra ⅛″–³⁄₁₆″ does the trick.

Joy

Joy comes to us in moments—ordinary moments. We risk missing out on joy when we get too busy chasing down the extraordinary.

—Brené Brown

Baby Clothes Quilt

TASHA + IZAIAH

Tasha is an early childhood educator. Her son, Izaiah, is a spunky, talkative, and lovable boy—and the love of her life.

On defining moments and becoming a mother

Putting the clothing together for the quilt was nice. It's hard to remember that he was *that* small—you almost forget.

A defining moment with the clothing: Coming home with Izaiah from the hospital. All of a sudden, I was responsible for a human being. Motherhood was a new chapter in my life.

When Izaiah was two weeks old, he developed meningitis, and we had to stay in the hospital. I remember the doctor saying, "We'll do our best." It was the hardest week and a half of my entire life.

That experience amplifies my feelings about the clothing. When I look at these items and see all his milestones … he beat the odds and pulled through. And now, to know those milestones are captured in this quilt …

Izaiah's baby overalls used in the quilt

The sense of smell is closely linked with memory and emotion.

The role of smell in memory keeping

When I gathered the clothing, I smelled every item. I felt joy but also choked up. Some things I want to keep in their full form. But what brought me comfort is the knowledge that I'm still going to have the clothes, but in a new form. It was okay to let go.

When I think about a quilt, I think about comfort and warmth. When your kid is all grown up, they can still be your baby when you hold that quilt. It's different than photographs because I can smell and hold the clothing and memories. I can imagine holding the quilt and smelling and thinking back: "Oh, remember that time … ?"

Tasha's many emotions upon receiving her quilt

About emotional hoarding + letting go

It's always been difficult for me to let go of sentimental things. I had been holding onto practically all of Izaiah's clothing until my mom said, "Time to let go. You can keep some things, but it's starting to get crowded." It was a good kind of release, though bittersweet. Having Izaiah's clothing made into a quilt is a perfect idea.

On storytelling and family history

This quilt will go in my archives of sentimental memories. I can't wait to share it with Izaiah and answer his questions, like "When was this?" and "Oh, you must have loved that, Mom … were you happy about that?" and "Do you need a hug?"

The quilt is a history that Izaiah can share with his family when he gets older. I'm so happy to start that history.

Tasha + Izaiah: Arabesque Tiles

Finished quilt: 44″ × 59″

Materials

Yardages are based on 40″ usable width, except where noted. Refer to Preparing Clothing for Quilting (page 22) to prepare the clothing fabric listed below before cutting it. Clothing quantities are approximate.

FOR ARABESQUE "TILES": 24 pieces of clothing, *each* providing:

　1 square 5½″ × 5½″

　8 squares 3″ × 3″

FOR OMBRÉ BACKGROUND: ⅝ yard *each* of:

FABRIC A: Extra light

FABRIC B: Light

FABRIC C: Medium

FABRIC D: Dark

FABRIC E: Extra dark

Fabric: Best for thin to medium fabric and non-shifting fabric

BACKING: 3 yards

BATTING: 52″ × 67″

BINDING: ½ yard

TEMPLATE MATERIAL, such as Visi-GRID Quilter's Template Sheets (by C&T Publishing; *optional*)

ESSENTIAL CIRCLE TOOL (by C&T Publishing; *optional*)

FAST2CUT SIMPLE SQUARE TEMPLATES (by C&T Publishing; *optional*)

Cutting

Using the convex circle and concave circle patterns (pullout page P2), trace and cut templates from template material. Note: If you are using the Essential Circle Tool, you do not need to make templates.

Measure twice + cut once!

CLOTHING ARABESQUES

From each of the 24 pieces of clothing, cut:

• 1 square 5½″ × 5½″

• 8 squares 3″ × 3″

NOTE | Using Small Clothing

If you are using baby clothes and can't cut all of the pieces out of one piece of clothing, take a look at the patterns for the convex and concave pieces. You may be able to use partial squares. You can also substitute some of the 3″ × 3″ squares with another piece of clothing or quilting cotton of a similar color and value. Low-volume prints also work nicely, providing a softer patchwork feeling.

Tip: Build As You Go

When planning the fabric layout for this quilt, I like to build as I go, first cutting the 5½″ × 5½″ and 3″ × 3″ squares. I then determine the layout of the 5½″ × 5½″ focal squares and cut the convex and concave quarter-circles from the 3″ × 3″ squares to correspond to their focal center square, being cognizant of the surrounding background colors.

Cutting continued on page 34

OMBRÉ BACKGROUND

From each of Fabrics A and E, cut:

- 2 rectangles 5½″ × 8″
- 2 squares 5½″ × 5½″
- 18 squares 3″ × 3″
- 2 rectangles 2½″ × 28″
- 2 rectangles 2½″ × 7½″

From each of Fabrics B, C, and D, cut:

- 60 squares 3″ × 3″
- 2 rectangles 2½″ × 10½″

QUARTER-CIRCLES

After determining the layout of the clothing 5½″ × 5½″ squares, use the templates or ruler to cut the convex and concave circles following the Quarter-Circle Cutting chart (below). If using directional fabric, note the correct placement of the convex and concave circles. If using the Essential Circle Tool, place the center hole ¼″ up the left side of the square; cut the convex pieces on the 5½″ line and the concave pieces on the 4½″ line. The remainder of the 3″ × 3″ squares will be used whole.

Tip: Labeling

Labeling can seem like a tedious extra step, but it can save time in the long run. Considering the number of pieces and the fact that half of the arabesques are split up between 5 different blocks, labeling is recommended for this quilt. At minimum, labeling the clothing quarter-circle blocks of Tiles 4–7, 11–14, and 18–21 is helpful in minimizing placement errors.

QUARTER-CIRCLE CUTTING

Tile number	Fabric	# of convex circles (cut from 3″ × 3″ squares) per tile	# of concave circles (cut from 3″ × 3″ squares) per tile
All tiles	Clothing	4	4
1 and 22	Fabric B	6	4
8 and 15	Fabric B	8	4
2 and 23	Fabric C	6	4
9 and 16	Fabric C	8	4
3 and 24	Fabric D	6	4
10 and 17	Fabric D	8	4
4, 11, and 18	Fabric A	—	2
	Fabric B	—	2
5, 12, and 19	Fabric B	—	2
	Fabric C	—	2
6, 13, and 20	Fabric C	—	2
	Fabric D	—	2
7, 14, and 21	Fabric D	—	2
	Fabric E	—	2
Left corner and side blocks	Fabric A	6	—
Right corner and side blocks	Fabric E	6	—

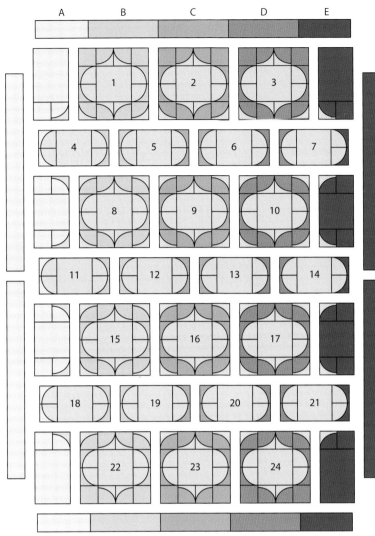

Quilt assembly

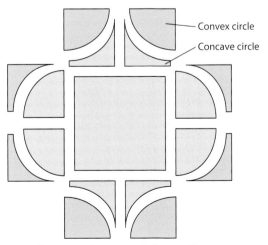

Convex and concave circles per tile

Piecing

Seam allowances are ¼″ unless otherwise noted. Nesting seams when pressing is recommended. Refer to the quilt assembly diagram (page 35) as needed.

This quilt is made up of 4 main blocks: the Corner block, the 10″ × 10″ Arabesque block, the 10″ × 5″ Arabesque block, and the Side block.

CORNER BLOCK

1. With right sides together, sew together 1 convex fabric A and 1 concave clothing quarter-circle piece from Tile 4, following the 5″ × 10″ Corner block diagram (at right). Press the seams toward Fabric A so that the clothing fabric lies flat.

2. Sew the 3″ × 3″ Fabric A cotton square to the left of the pieced quarter-circle, as shown. Press the seams open.

3. Sew the 5½″ × 8″ Fabric A rectangle to the top of the piece created in Step 2. Press the seams open. **(A)**

4. Repeat Steps 1–3 for the bottom left corner, but make sure to sew the quarter-circle block on the *right* side of the cotton square and the 3″ × 3″ squares to the top of the 5½″ × 8″ rectangle.

5. Repeat Steps 1–4 to make the right-side Corner blocks with Fabric E.

A

5″ × 10″ Corner block

10″ × 10″ ARABESQUE BLOCK

1. With *right sides together*, sew together 1 convex quarter-circle piece and 1 concave quarter-circle piece to make a quarter-circle segment. Press the seams toward the quilting cotton so the clothing fabric lies flat. Make 10 quarter-circle segments for Blocks 1–3 and 22–24, and 12 segments for Blocks 8–10 and 15–17.

2. With right sides together, sew together 2 quarter-circle segments from Step 1 to create the arabesque top peak, as shown. *Note:* The peaks should come to a point—if they finish with a blunt edge, they are sewn together incorrectly. Make 2. **(B)**

3. With right sides together, sew together 2 quarter-circle segments from Step 1 to create a side half-circle. Press the seams open. Make 2. **(C)**

4. Refer to the piecing diagrams (next page) to assemble the Arabesque block columns.

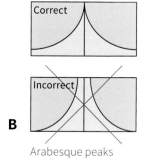

B

Arabesque peaks

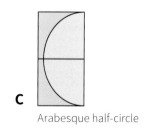

C

Arabesque half-circle

FOR BLOCKS 1–3: Sew a 3″ × 3″ square to the top side of a half-circle and a quarter-circle block to the bottom side. Press the seams open. Make 2. **(D)**

FOR BLOCKS 22–24: Sew a quarter-circle block to the top side of a half-circle and a 3″ × 3″ square to the bottom side. Make 2.

FOR BLOCKS 8–10 AND 15–17: Sew a quarter-circle block to both the top and bottom side of the half-circle. Press all seams open. Make 2. **(E)**

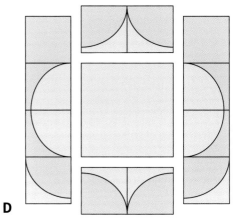

D

Piecing the Arabesque blocks 1–3

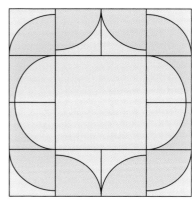

E

Piecing the Arabesque blocks 8–10 and 15–17

5. Sew the peaks created in Step 2 to the top and bottom of the 5½″ × 5½″ clothing square, as shown. Press the seams open.

6. Sew together the columns created in Steps 3–5, as shown. Press the seams open.

7. Repeat Steps 1–6 to make Blocks 1–3, 8–10, 15–17, and 22–24. **(F)**

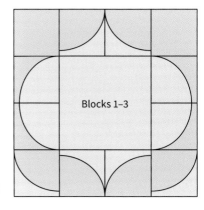

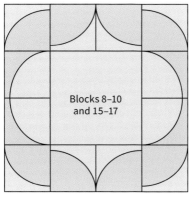

Blocks 1–3

Blocks 8–10 and 15–17

Blocks 22–24

F

10″ × 10″ Arabesque block variations

10″ × 5″ ARABESQUE BLOCK

1. With right sides together, sew together 1 convex clothing quarter-circle piece and 1 concave quilting-cotton quarter-circle piece. Press the seams toward the quilting cotton so that clothing fabric lies flat.

2. Repeat Step 1 make a total of 4 quarter-circle blocks. Note that the 2 pieces of the quilting cotton on the left are a different color than the ones on the right.

3. With right sides together, sew together 2 quarter-circle blocks created in Step 1 to create the left-side half-circle, as shown. The 2 quarter-circle blocks should have the same quilting cotton color. Press all seams open. Repeat with 2 blocks of a different color of quilting cotton to create the right-side half-circle. (G)

4. Sew the half-circles to the 5½″ × 5½″ clothing square, as shown. Press the seams open.

5. Repeat Steps 1–4 to make a total of 12 Arabesque blocks 10″ × 5″. (H)

SIDE BLOCK

1. With right sides together, sew together 1 convex Fabric A piece and 1 concave clothing quarter-circle piece, being sure to coordinate the correct clothing piece for the location of the block. Press the seams toward Fabric A so that the clothing fabric lies flat. Repeat to create the second quarter-circle block.

2. Sew the 3″ × 3″ Fabric A squares to the pieced quarter-circles, as shown. Press the seams open.

3. Sew the 5½″ × 5½″ Fabric A square to the pieces created in Step 2. Press the seams open.

4. Repeat Steps 1–3 for a second Side block in Fabric A and 2 Side blocks in Fabric E, being mindful of placement and clothing, to make a total of 4 Side blocks. (I)

QUILT TOP ASSEMBLY

1. Sew together the pieced blocks by rows. Press the seams open.

2. Sew together the rows. Press the seams open.

3. Sew together the left, right, top, and bottom border pieces. Press the seams open.

4. Sew the left and right borders to the quilt top. Press the seams open.

5. Sew the top and bottom borders to the quilt top. Ombré cotton colors should align with the pieced Arabesque blocks. Press the seams open.

6. Square and trim the quilt top to 44½″ × 59½″.

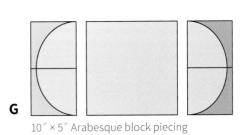

G

10″ × 5″ Arabesque block piecing

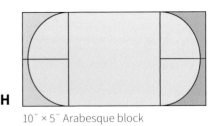

H

10″ × 5″ Arabesque block

I

5″ × 10″ Side block

Finishing

Layer the quilt top, batting, and backing to make a quilt sandwich.
Baste, quilt, and bind using your preferred methods.

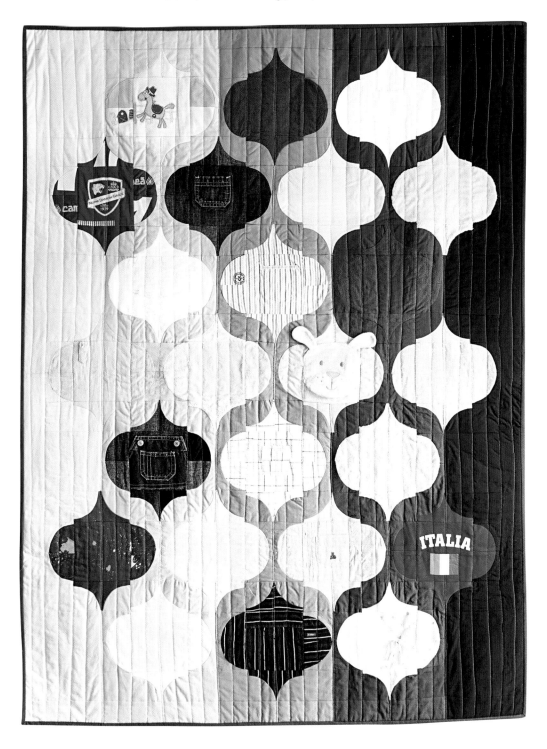

Twin Quilts

JACQUELINE, STELLA + FELIX

Jacqueline is mama to twins Stella and Felix and the owner of Soak Wash, Inc. She loves to sew quilts, clothing, and lots of baby things.

On Stella + Felix and the importance of quilts

Stella and Felix are fraternal twins who are always smiling. And they are already wearing lots of handmade clothing. I love that I'm their mama!

Quilts are a really important part of our lives. We always have one laid out in the living room like a rug so the babies have somewhere they know is theirs. The story of the parts and people that make a quilt is important—you can constantly revisit and learn from it.

Jacqueline, Felix + Stella

On memory keeping

At the time, it's hard to tell whether something is important. I didn't realize a couple things were important until I had already given them away. You think, "I can live without these secondhand pajamas." But then, "I'll never get back those pajamas that the babies wore!"

It's not until you see a picture or a memory of something later that you realize its importance. I started keeping more and filtering out after.

About the clothing

The clothing represents a transition from not having babies and really wanting them to having them as part of our lives. We had a really hard time getting pregnant—but then we had *two* babies!

Liberty of London shirt: I bought this after my last miscarriage, trying to figure out what I was going to do with the whole idea of maybe not having children. It will look lovely, and it is important yet sad—it will always remind me of that time period.

My dad's shirt: He is the oldest of all the grandparents and just loves the babies. I'm terrified of the day when he won't be there anymore. I wanted a piece of him included.

First baby clothes: I wanted to include preemie onesies for scale. Some of the twins' first pajamas and clothing are also included. My first post-baby sewing project was making swaddle blankets out of flannel, so there are some scraps in there.

How quilts are different from photos

Quilts are tactile and repurposed; that's unique. It's allowing something to have a new life but also allowing it to die, because if you use a quilt, it eventually wears out. It's not so precious that it has to be preserved and can never be touched or ruined.

On legacy

I want Stella and Felix to know how many people love them—like a blanket of insurance for them to feel the warmth of the people in their lives. One day, my parents won't be around, and I might not be around. It's important to know the stories of the pieces, because you have no idea how fragile life is and when it will be too late to know.

It's important to understand the community that comes from the handmade element of gifting and sharing. You learn that through quilts.

Photos 1-2 and 4-5 by Jacqueline Sava; Photo 3 by Karyn Valino

Stella + Felix's community of love

Jacqueline, Stella + Felix: Animal Silhouettes

Finished quilt: 36″ × 52″

Materials

Yardages are based on 40″ usable width, except where noted. Refer to Preparing Clothing for Quilting (page 22) to prepare the clothing fabric listed below before cutting it. Clothing quantities are approximate.

Note: *The instructions make one quilt. If you would like to make both twin quilts, make this project twice and use a different animal appliqué pattern each time.*

Fabric: Good for most. Recommended for baby clothing.

QUILTING COTTON:

FABRIC A: 1½ yards of white for background

FABRIC B: ⅓ yard of black or dark fabric for contrast

FABRIC C: ¾ yard for appliqué

CLOTHING: Approximately 15–36 baby or small-child clothing pieces *or* 6–12 adult clothing pieces

BACKING: 2½ yards

BATTING: 44″ × 60″

BINDING: ½ yard

NONPERMANENT MARKING TOOL, such as a Hera Marker

TEMPLATE MATERIAL, such as Visi-GRID Quilter's Template Sheets (by C&T Publishing), *or* **PRINTER PAPER**

Tip: Baby-Clothing Friendly

The band of rectangles on the right of this quilt is great for incorporating a lot of different pieces of clothing. And the diminutive size (1½″ × 3″) of the rectangles means that the small-scale prints on baby clothes fit perfectly. You can also cut larger pieces if you choose, as I did.

Cutting

Enlarge by 400% the rhinoceros or bird pattern (pullout page P1), or download the full-size pattern from tinyurl.com/11266-patterns-download. Trace and cut a template from the taped-together template material or printer paper.

Measure twice + cut once!

QUILTING COTTON

From Fabric A, cut:

• 1 half-square triangle 10⅞″ × 10⅞″ (A1)

• 1 rectangle 3½″ × 2¼″ (A2) and 1 square 2¾″ × 2¾″. Subcut into 2 half-square triangles (A2a, A2b).

• 1 rectangle 3½″ × 10½″ (A3)

Cutting continued on page 44

- 1 half-square triangle 11″ × 11″ (A4)

- 1 rectangle 2¾″ × 12½″ (A5)

- 1 rectangle 3″ × 5″ (A6) and 1 square 3½″ × 3½″. Subcut into 2 half-square triangles (A6a, A6b).

- 1 rectangle 2¾″ × 10″ (A7) and 1 half-square triangle 3¼″ × 3¼″ (A7a)

- 1 rectangle 4½″ × 12¼″ (A8) and 1 half-square triangle 5″ × 5″ (A8a)

- 1 rectangle 8⅜″ × 24¼″ (A9) and 1 half-square triangle 8⅞″ × 8⅞″ (A9a)

- 1 rectangle 7¾″ × 27″ (A10) and 1 half-square triangle 8¼″ × 8¼″ (A10a)

- 1 half-square triangle 19¾″ × 19¾″ (A11)

- 4 squares 6″ × 6″. Subcut into 8 half-square triangles (A12, A13, A13a, A14a, A14b, A15a, A15b, A16a).

- 1 rectangle 1¼″ × 5½″ (A14)

- 1 rectangle 5½″ × 6⅜″ (A15)

- 1 rectangle 5½″ × 13⅛″ (A16)

- 1 half-square triangle 8″ × 8″ (A17)

From Fabric B, cut:

- 2 strips 1¾″ × width of fabric. Subcut into 19 rectangles 1¾″ × 3½″ (B1).

- 1 strip 2¼″ × 40″ (B2a)

- 1 strip 2¼″ × 13″ (B2b)

From Fabric C:

Using either the rhinoceros *or* bird template, trace and cut the animal silhouette out of Fabric C. If you would like to needle-turn appliqué the silhouette, be sure to add your preferred seam allowance before you cut it out.

FROM CLOTHING, CUT:

- 1 rectangle 3″ × 9½″ (C1) and 1 half-square triangle 3½″ × 3½″ (C1a)

- 1 half-square triangle 6½″ × 6½″ (C2)

- 1 rectangle 2¼″ × 5¾″ (C3) and 1 half-square triangle 2¾″ × 2¾″ (C3a)

- 1 rectangle 2¼″ × 15″ (C4) and 1 half-square triangle 2¾″ × 2¾″ (C4a)

- 1 rectangle 3″ × 15″ (C5), 1 rectangle 3″ × 2¾″ (C5a), and 1 half-square triangle 3½″ × 3½″ (C5b)

- 1 rectangle 2¼″ × 10½″ (C6) and 1 square 2¾″ × 2¾″. Subcut into 2 half-square triangles (C6a, C6b).

- 1 rectangle 3″ × 10½″ (C7)

- 1 rectangle 2¼″ × 24⅛″ (C8), 1 rectangle 2¼″ × 12¼″ (C8b), and 2 half-square triangles 2¾″ × 2¾″ (C8a, C8c)

- 1 rectangle 2¼″ × 24″ (C9) and 1 square 2¾″ × 2¾″. Subcut into 2 half-square triangles (C9a, C9b).

- 1 rectangle 2¼″ × 10½″ (C10) and 1 square 2¾″ × 2¾″. Subcut into 2 half-square triangles (C10a, C10b).

- 1 rectangle 2½″ × 4½″ (C11) and 1 half-square triangle 3″ × 3″ (C11a)

- 1 rectangle 2½″ × 10¼″ (C12) and 1 square 3″ × 3″. Subcut into 2 half-square triangles (C12a, C12b).

- 1 rectangle 2½″ × 5¾″ (C13) and 1 half-square triangle 3″ × 3″ (C13a)

- 1 rectangle 2″ × 22¾″ (C14) and 1 half-square triangle 2½″ × 2½″ (C14a)

- 1 rectangle 2″ × 21¼″ (C15) and 1 half-square triangle 2½″ × 2½″ (C15a)

- 1 rectangle 2″ × 19¾″ (C16) and 1 half-square triangle 2½″ × 2½″ (C16a)

- 1 rectangle 2″ × 18¼″ (C17) and 1 half-square triangle 2½″ × 2½″ (C17a)

- 5 rectangles 2¼″ × 10½″ (C18, C19, C20, C21, C23)

- 1 rectangle 3″ × 11″ (C22)

- 19 rectangles 2″ × 3½″ (C24)

Piecing

Seam allowances are ¼″ unless otherwise noted. Refer to the quilt assembly diagram (page 49) as needed.

LEFT MAIN BLOCK

Press the seams open and trim the corners after every step.

Section 1

Refer to the Section 1 assembly diagram (page 46) as needed.

BLOCK 1

1. Sew piece C13a to C13 and piece A10 to A10a.

2. Sew piece C13/C13a to piece A10/A10a.

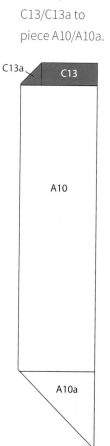

BLOCK 2

Sew piece A9 to piece A9a.

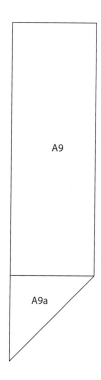

BLOCK 3

1. Sew piece C14 to C14a. Repeat for C15/C15a, C16/C16a, and C17/C17a.

2. Sew together the pieces created in Step 1.

BLOCK 4

1. Sew together pieces C11, A8, and A8a.

2. Sew together pieces C11a and C12a. Sew together pieces C12 and C12b.

3. Sew together the pieces created in Step 2.

4. Sew together pieces C10 and C10b.

5. Sew together the pieces created in Steps 1, 3, and 4.

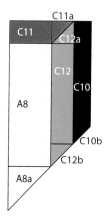

BLOCK 5

1. Sew together pieces C8 and C8a.

2. Sew together pieces C9b and C10a.
Sew together pieces C9 and C9a.

3. Sew together the pieces created in Step 2.

4. Sew together the pieces created in Steps 1 and 3.

SECTION 1 ASSEMBLY (A)

1. Sew together Blocks 1 and 2 as shown. Trim the overhanging part of piece A10a as shown. **(B)**

2. Sew together piece A11 and Blocks 1/2 (created in Step 1), 3, and 4, as shown.

3. Sew Block 5 to the piece created in Step 2.

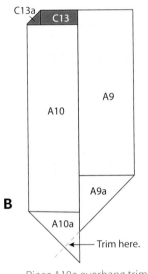

Piece A10a overhang trim

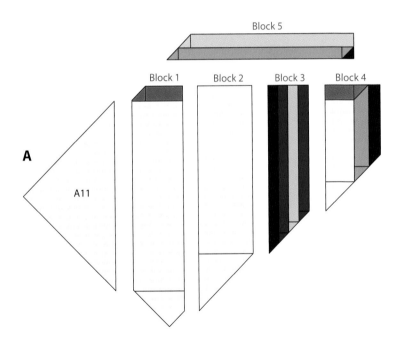

Section 2

BLOCK 6

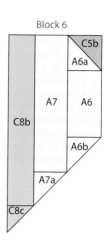

Block 6

1. Sew together pieces C8b and C8c.

2. Sew together pieces A7 and A7a.

3. Sew together pieces C5b and A6a. Sew together pieces A6 and A6a.

4. Sew together the pieces created in Step 3.

5. Sew together the pieces created in Steps 1, 2, and 4.

Section 3

Refer to the Section 3 assembly diagram (below right) as needed.

BLOCK 7

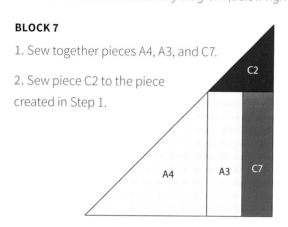

1. Sew together pieces A4, A3, and C7.

2. Sew piece C2 to the piece created in Step 1.

BLOCK 8

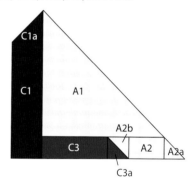

1. Sew together pieces C3, C3a, A2b, A2, and A2a.

2. Sew piece A1 to the piece created in Step 1.

3. Sew piece C1 to C1a.

4. Sew the piece created in Step 3 to the piece created in Step 2.

BLOCK 9

1. Sew piece A5 to C5a.

2. Sew the piece created in Step 1 to pieces C5 and C4.

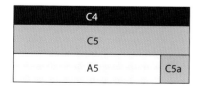

SECTION 3 ASSEMBLY

1. Sew Block 8 to Block 9.

2. Sew Block 7 to Block 8/9.

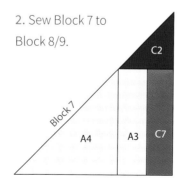

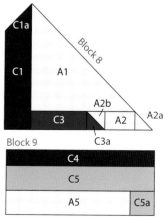

Section 4

BLOCK 10

1. Sew piece C4a to C6a and piece C6 to C6b.

2. Sew together the pieces created in Step 1.

3. Sew piece A17 to the piece created in Step 2, taking care to align as shown.

4. Trim triangles C4a and C6a even with A17.

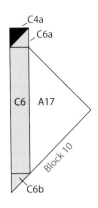

Sections 1–4 Assembly

1. Sew Section 1 to Section 2.

2. Sew Section 3 to Section 1/2.

3. Sew Section 4 to Section 1/2/3.

4. Press, square, and trim the Left Main block to 26½″ × 52½″. **(A)**

RIGHT MAIN BLOCK (B)

Press the seams open and trim the corners after every step.

1. Using a nonpermanent marking tool, mark the center point on the long edges of the following blocks: A12, A13, A13a, A14a, A14b, A15a, A15b, and A16a. For rectangles C18, C19, and C23, mark 4¼″ from each short edge. For C21, mark 3¼″ from both short edges, and for C22, mark 3½″ from the right short edge and 4½″ from the left short edge.

2. Matching the marked points as shown, sew together A12, C18, and A13. Trim to 5½″ × 8″.

3. Repeat Step 2 with pieces A13a, C19, and A14a.

4. Repeat Step 2 with pieces A15b, C23, and A16a.

5. Matching the marked points, sew together pieces A14b, C20, C21, C22, and A15a. Trim to 5½″ × 13¾″.

6. Sew together the blocks created in Steps 2–5 with pieces A14, A15, and A16, as shown.

7. Press and trim the Right Main block to 5½″ × 52½″.

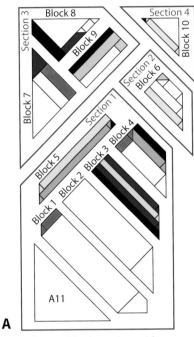

A

Left Main block piecing guide

CENTER STRIPED BLOCK (C)

1. Starting with a B1 rectangle (1¾″ × 3½″), sew together alternating B1 and C24 rectangles (2″ × 3½″).

2. Sew the B2a rectangle (2¼″ × 40″) to the B2b rectangle (2¼″ × 13″).

3. Sew the strip made in Step 1 to the B2 strip, aligning the lower edges.

4. Trim the Center Striped block to 5¼″ × 52½″.

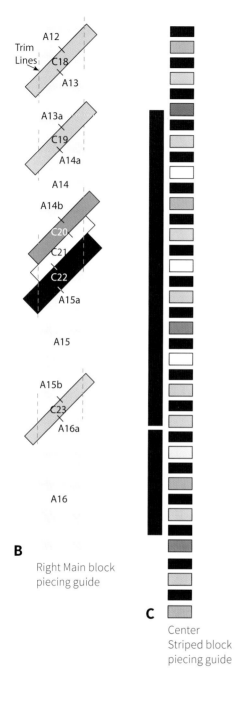

Trim Lines

B

Right Main block piecing guide

C

Center Striped block piecing guide

QUILT TOP ASSEMBLY

1. Pin and sew together the Left Main block, Center Striped block, and Right Main block as shown.

2. Press and trim the quilt top to 36½″ × 52½″.

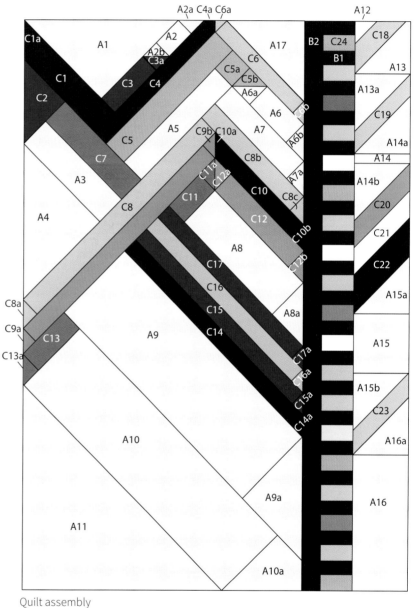

Quilt assembly

Finishing

APPLIQUÉ

Position the animal appliqué; pin and baste it into place. For machine appliqué, edgestitch around the perimeter of the silhouette using a zigzag, blanket, or other stitch. For raw-edge appliqué, use a straight stitch.

Layer the quilt top, batting, and backing to make a quilt sandwich. Baste, quilt, and bind using your preferred methods.

Personalization: Embroidery Detail

A hand-embroidered message is a great way to personalize a memory quilt. For Stella and Felix, I added a message to remind them of the love in their family and community.

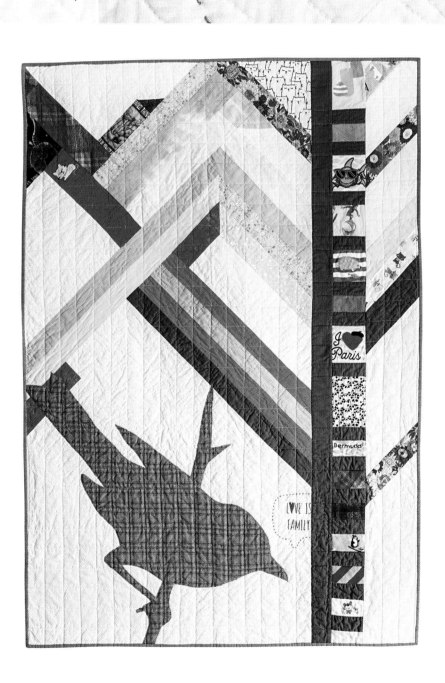

First Years Quilt

VIVIAN + LUCAS

*Vivian is a portrait photographer,
all-around creative person, and
mom to Lucas—the light of her life.*

About Lucas and motherhood

I wanted to be a mother for so long, and it took us a long time to get here. He really is a treasure. I tell him that he is the gift the universe gave me.

Lucas is a sensitive, imaginative, funny, and kind little guy. He always wants hugs and cuddles and is very intuitive about when you aren't feeling well.

The happiest I ever was was when I knew that I was going to have this baby. Being his mom has just been a joy.

Hexies made from Lucas's clothes

On the meaning behind the clothing and dressing a small child

As a creative person, part of the dream of being a mother is to combine colors and patterns to come up with a cute outfit for your child. Seeing these clothes that I carefully selected reminds me of this phase of his life. It's a celebration of the act of dressing your child—and of motherhood.

On defining moments

Finding out I was pregnant with Lucas was a defining moment—the beginning of my relationship with him. The day that his father left, Lucas and I had this moment where we looked at each other, knowing that life was going to be different but that together we would be okay. It was profound and sad yet enlightening.

There are so many moments together: everything we've celebrated, trips that we've taken, love that we've shared.

Love is a daily practice. It's what makes up your life. If every day has love in it, then you'll have a life of love.

What feels like love? Careful attention every day.

And letting go

At my age, I know I'm not going to have another baby. It's difficult to let go of these clothes, knowing in my heart that I am letting go of the idea of having another kid.

The fact that we will get to see the clothes every day, draped on a couch or on a bed, is really nice. The clothes leave the house temporarily, but they come back reincarnated.

Photography and quilts as memory keeping

It will be really nice for Lucas to see the photographs of the clothes and then see the piece of clothing in the quilt. I like the juxtaposition.

I wanted the quilt to be playful and fun, and to show a little bit of my style, a little bit of what we liked, and a lot of his personality.

On the importance of preserving memories in a quilt

It's my son, and the clothes represent a beautiful moment in my life. It's also a time that we were all still together as a family.

Vivian + Lucas: Ombré Hexies

Finished quilt: 60½″ × 72″

Materials

Yardages are based on 43″ usable width, except where noted. Refer to Preparing Clothing for Quilting (page 22) to prepare the clothing fabric listed below before cutting it. Clothing quantities are approximate.

Quilting cotton yardage amounts listed are for a usable width of 43″ and are the maximum quantities needed (that is, the amount needed to make the quilt solely in quilting cotton). Depending on how much clothing you use, your cotton requirements will vary, but they will not be more than the yardage listed.

You will need 288 half-hexagons total. The amount per color group has been rounded up to the same number of half-hexagons in each group.

Fabric: Good for all. Thick fabric and baby clothes friendly.

QUILTING COTTON:

FABRIC A (EXTRA LIGHT): ¾ yard

FABRIC B (LIGHT): ¾ yard

FABRIC C (LIGHT MEDIUM): ¾ yard

FABRIC D (MEDIUM): ¾ yard

FABRIC E (MEDIUM DARK): ¾ yard

FABRIC F (DARK): ¾ yard

FABRIC G (EXTRA DARK): ¾ yard

or

CLOTHING: 72–144 little-kid shirts, 15–24 bigger-kid shirts, *or* about 10 youth or adult shirts

BACKING: 4 yards

BATTING: 68″ × 80″

BINDING: ⅝ yard

TEMPLATE MATERIAL, such as Visi-GRID Quilter's Template Sheets (by C&T Publishing; *optional*)

HEX N MORE RULER (*optional*)

CALCULATING YARDAGE + CLOTHING REQUIRED

It is sometimes difficult to provide the total amount of fabric needed for a quilt made with clothing.

For this quilt, plan on getting 2–4 half-hexies from little-kid shirts or onesies (1–5 years old), 12–20 half-hexies from bigger-kid shirts (6–12 years old), and 30+ half-hexies from youth and adult shirts. (These amounts are based on using the front and back of the shirt but not the sleeves.)

For quilting cotton, a 3½″ × 43″ width-of-fabric strip will give you 7 half-hexagons.

Cutting

Using the half-hexagon pattern (pullout page P2), trace and cut a template from template material. If you are using the Hex N More ruler, you do not need to make a template.

Measure twice + cut once!

HALF-HEXAGONS

Using the template or a Hex N More ruler, cut 42 half-hexagons 7½″ × 3½″ from each of Fabrics A, B, C, D, E, F, and G *or* clothing. For the Hex N More ruler, cut along the 6½″ Half Hex lines.

Tip: Whole-Hexagon Appliqués

When designing this quilt, I found a few appliqués and prints on Lucas's clothing that I wanted to keep whole and use as focal points. I cut them as whole hexagons (7¼″ × 6¼″) and machine appliquéd them on top (with the edges left raw) before I sandwiched and completed the quilt. Cutting the hexagons slightly larger than the finished size hides the fabric underneath when the raw edges roll.

Tip: Color Group Proportions

Cut about 30–35 half-hexagons of each color group and start laying them out on a design wall. You may discover an effect that works well and decide to alter the proportions of the color groups to enhance it.

Piecing

Seam allowances are ¼″ unless otherwise noted. Refer to the quilt assembly diagram (page 58) as needed.

PLANNING *the* OMBRÉ DESIGN

1. Starting from the top or bottom, build ombré half-hexagon layers for the quilt. The full quilt is 12 half-hexagons wide and 24 rows in length. Follow the quilt assembly diagram (page 58) to give a sense of movement to the quilt, or arrange the hexagons as desired.

2. When you have an arrangement you like, snap a photo for reference.

QUILT TOP ASSEMBLY

1. Starting at the top, number each row with tape on the left hexagon of each row.

2. Working one row at a time, pin together the hexagons the way you will sew them, with right sides together. Pin one seam at a time, always returning to the design wall to ensure you keep the proper order. Remove the pinned row from the design wall.

3. Sew together all hexagon side seams, and press the seams open.

4. Return the sewn and pressed rows to the design wall in the proper order.

5. Sew together 2 rows at a time until you end up with 12 strips. Be sure to match all seam intersections as you sew.

6. Continue in this manner, sewing together 2 strips at a time, until the quilt top is completed. Press the seams open.

7. If you are adding any full hexagon appliqués, place them now and hand or machine stitch them in place.

Quilt assembly

Finishing

1. Trim the sides of the quilt top even with the inner points.

2. Layer the quilt top, batting, and backing to make a quilt sandwich. Baste, quilt, and bind using your preferred methods.

Wedding Quilt

JEFFREY + CLAY

Jeffrey and Clay were born in very small rural towns in Manitoba and Ontario but have lived in Toronto for many years. They both love living in a large, creative city. Their childhood homes have given them a great appreciation of the country and nature.

Jeffrey (with beagle Winston by his side) met Clay in 2003 on a blind date over coffee. Winston was so excited to meet Clay that he peed in his lap. On January 2, 2014, Jeffrey and Clay were married—10 years to the day of that first date. This quilt is part wedding quilt, part homage to Winston.

Photo by Karyn Valino

About the proposal ...

JEFFREY: I proposed to Clay after a midnight walk on Christmas Eve with a chocolate cake, a bottle of champagne, and my father's wedding ring.

... and the wedding day

JEFFREY: The wedding venue was at a local craft brewery. We had our own beer created for the party, with a custom label for the bottles designed by Clay. Winston wasn't allowed in the wedding venue, but we brought a framed photo from our annual family shoot with Santa from a few weeks earlier as a placeholder.

CLAY: We both love baking, so we hosted a party with our newly combined family and baked an entire table full of our favorite recipes.

Jeffrey, Clay + Winston with Santa

Photo by The Pawsway, Toronto

MODERN MEMORY QUILTS

About the clothing in the quilt

JEFFREY: The clothing is from our beloved beagle, Winston, as well as from our own closets. After Winston passed, we packed up his clothing because we felt we couldn't just throw it out ... and it was too well loved (and covered in beagle hair) to donate.

Pulling out all Winston's clothing after two years brought back a lot of good memories. We knew a quilt was the right way to honor his memory and the perfect way to remember our best friend who nightly stole the covers from us in bed. Winston was a big part of our relationship, and his rugby shirt was the anchor and starting point for our clothing selections.

CLAY: The articles of our own clothing include Jeffrey's Death Records T-shirt from his favorite movie. There is a pair of matching camouflage dress shirts we wore to a friend's wedding. We frequently visit New York City, and many of the shirts are from vacations to the Big Apple.

These shirts encapsulate who we are: some fashion pieces and many ironic and iconic black T-shirts, peppered with dog clothing.

About Winston

CLAY: Winston was charismatic, adorable, spoiled, destructive, and too smart for his own good. He had a sixth sense about when we were about to leave the apartment and would run for his leash because he didn't want us out of his sight. There was no "dog-proofing" that Winston couldn't think his way through. We suspect he might have been able to fly but never witnessed it personally.

On capturing moments

JEFFREY: We lost Winston two years ago, and though we have many photos of him, we've always wanted to create something special in his memory. We didn't want something that reminded us of losing him but instead of the happy times we spent together. Having an object we interact with everyday means he'll always be part of our lives in a very tangible way.

Photo by Clay Mullen

On favorite memories

CLAY: Lazy afternoons were often spent as a family curled up on the couch in front of the television, buried under a blanket. We felt like a quilt made from some of Winston's and our clothes from this period of time would be a wonderful way to remember those relaxing afternoons.

Jeffrey + Clay: Intersections

Finished quilt: 50″ × 50″

Materials

Yardages are based on 40″ usable width, except where noted. Refer to Preparing Clothing for Quilting (page 22) to prepare the clothing fabric listed below before cutting it. Clothing quantities are approximate.

QUILTING COTTON:

FABRIC A (WHITE): ⅝ yard

FABRIC B (BLACK): ¼ yard

FABRIC C (RED): 1⅜ yards

FABRIC D (YELLOW): ⅛ yard

Fabric: Best for adult clothing or large pieces of fabric.

CLOTHING: Approximately 10–12 adult clothing pieces *or* 24–36 baby or small-child clothing pieces

BACKING: 3¼ yards

BATTING: 58″ × 58″

BINDING: ½ yard

NONPERMANENT MARKING TOOL, such as a Hera Marker

Tip: Oversized Piecing

This project contains several blocks that are larger than most pieces of clothing. To create a color-blocked effect, combine several pieces of clothing of a similar background color. Improv piece them together or use a simple grid pattern; then cut the oversize block. If you don't have enough clothing, substitute with quilting cotton.

Cutting

Measure twice + cut once!

QUILTING COTTON

From Fabric A, cut:

- 3 rectangles 3½″ × 17½″ (A1)
- 5 strips 1½″ × 26½″ (B2)

From Fabric B, cut:

- 5 strips 1½″ × 36½″ (B1)

From Fabric C, cut:

- 13 strips 1″ × 40″ (E1)

- 6 strips 1″ × 36½″ (B1)
- 6 strips 1″ × 26½″ (B2)
- 12 strips 1″ × 25½″ (B2/C3)
- 3 strips 1¼″ × 25¼″ (C4/D3)
- 2 strips 1¼″ × 17½″ (A1)

From Fabric D, cut:

- 1 strip 1¼″ × 25¼″

CLOTHING

Cut the following from clothing, piecing clothing together when necessary (see Oversized Piecing, below left):

- 1 rectangle 17½″ × 33½″ (A2)
- 1 rectangle 17½″ × 29½″ (C1)
- 1 rectangle 7¼″ × 17½″ (C2)
- 1 rectangle 17½″ × 21″ (C4)
- 11 rectangles 1½″ × 17½″ (C3)
- 1 rectangle 20½″ × 20¾″ (D1)
- 1 rectangle 8¼″ × 13½″ (D2)
- 1 rectangle 8¼″ × 38″ (D3)
- 12 strips 1½″ × 40″ (E1)
- 2 strips 3½″ × 40″ (E1)

Piecing

Seam allowances are ¼″ unless otherwise noted. Refer to the quilt assembly diagram (page 66) as needed.

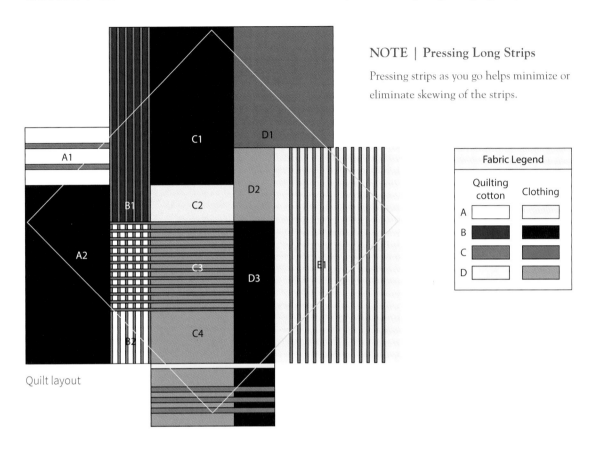

Quilt layout

Refer to the quilt assembly diagram (page 66) as needed.

NOTE | Pressing Long Strips

Pressing strips as you go helps minimize or eliminate skewing of the strips.

	Fabric Legend	
	Quilting cotton	Clothing
A		
B		
C		
D		

BLOCK A1

Sew together 3 rectangles 3½″ × 17½″ with 2 fabric C strips 1¼″ × 17½″, as shown. Press the seams open. Square and trim to 11″ × 17½″.

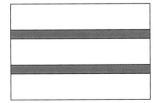

BLOCK B1

Sew together the 6 Fabric C 1″ × 36½″ strips with the 5 Fabric B 1½″ × 36½″ strips, as shown. Press the seams open. Square and trim to 8½″ × 36½″.

BLOCK B2

1. Sew together the 6 Fabric C strips 1″ × 26½″ with 5 Fabric A strips 1½″ × 26½″, as shown. Press the seams open. Square and trim to 8½″ × 26½″. **(A)**

2. Cut 11 strips 1½″ × 8½″ from the block made in Step 1, as shown. You will be left with 1 striped block 8½″ × 10″. **(B)**

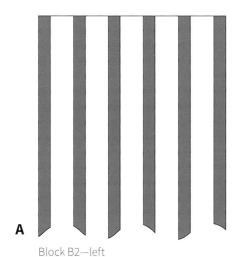

A

Block B2—left

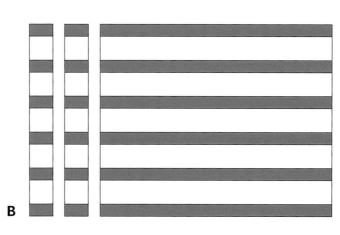

B

BLOCK B2 + C3/C4 ASSEMBLY

1. Sew a clothing C3 rectangle 1½″ × 17½″ to a 1½″ × 8½″ strip cut in Block B2, Step 2 (above). Repeat to make 11 B2/C3 rectangles. **(C)**

2. Sew the 8½″ × 10″ striped block from Block B2, Step 2 to the 17½″ × 21″ C4 rectangle as shown. **(D)**

3. Sew together the pieces created in Steps 1 and 2 with the 12 fabric C 1″ × 25½″ strips. Press the seams to one side. The block should measure 25½″ long and 38″ wide on the C3 side. **(E)**

C

D

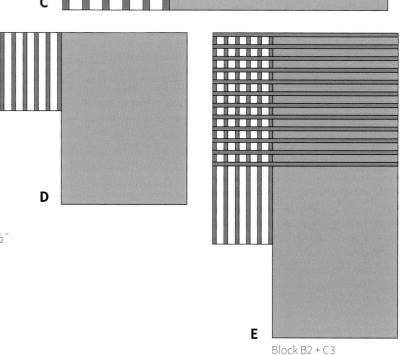

E

Block B2 + C3

BLOCK E1

1. Sew together 13 fabric C 1″ × 40″ and 12 clothing strips 1½″ × 40″. Start and finish with a fabric C strip. Press the seams to one side.

2. Sew a 3½″ × 40″ clothing strip on each side of the block created in Step 1. Press the seams open.

3. Press and trim to 25″ × 40″.

QUILT TOP ASSEMBLY

1. Sew Block A1 to Block A2. Press the seam open.

2. Sew Block C1 to Block C2. Press the seam open. Sew Block C1/C2 to Block B1, aligning the bottom edges of B1 and C2. Press the seam open.

3. Sew Block B1/C1/C2 to Block B2/C3/C4. Press the seam open.

4. Sew the block created in Step 3 to Block A1/A2, aligning the bottom edges of Block A2 and Block B2. Press the seam open.

5. Sew Block D2 to Block D3. Press the seams open. Sew Block D2/D3 to Block E1. Press the seam open.

6. Sew Block D2/D3/E1 to Block D1. Press the seam open.

7. Aligning the bottom edges of Blocks C4 and D3, sew together the blocks created in Steps 4 and 6. **(A)**

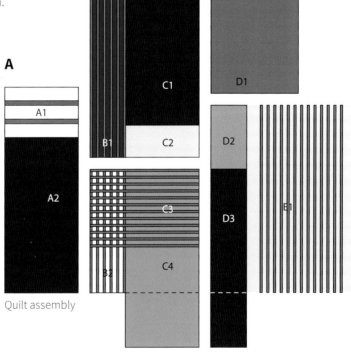

Quilt assembly

8. Using a nonpermanent marking tool, mark the lower edge of the overhanging piece C4/D3. Trim this piece off even with the lower edge of Blocks A2/B2 and E1.

9. Starting at the marked bottom end of the trimmed piece C4/D3, cut 1 strip 2¾″ × 25¼″ and 2 strips 1½″ × 25½″, as shown.

10. Sew the pieces cut in Step 9 with the 3 fabric C 1¼″ × 25¼″ strips and the fabric D 1¼″ × 25¼″ strip, as shown. Press the seams open. Trim. **(B)**

11. Sew the block back to the C4/D3 section of the quilt. Press the quilt top.

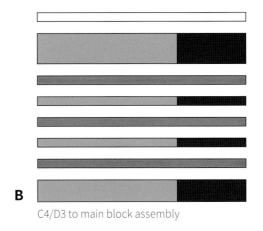

B

C4/D3 to main block assembly

TRIMMING *the* CENTRAL BLOCK ON POINT

1. Following the bottom edge of Block C2, use a marking tool to extend and trace a line parallel to the sides of the block (x-axis), shown in blue.

2. Measuring 5″ to the left of the D blocks, trace a line perpendicular to the x-axis to create the y-axis, shown in blue.

3. From the center, where the axes meet, measure 35¾″ toward the edge of the quilt top. Mark in all 4 directions along each axis. These will be the corner points of the central block. The measurement from diagonal point to point should be 71½″ in both directions.

4. Trace with a ruler and marker to connect the corner points. These will be the cutting lines (shown in yellow in the trimming diagram). The resulting square should measure 50½″ × 50½″.

5. Trim the quilt top. **(C)**

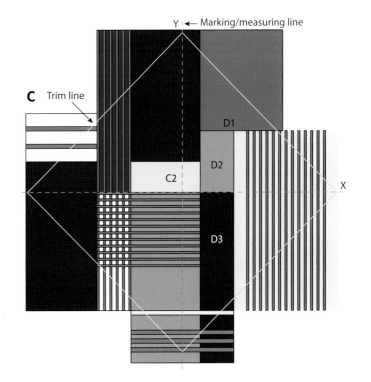

C Trim line

Finishing

Layer the quilt top, batting, and backing to make a quilt sandwich.
Baste, quilt, and bind using your preferred methods.

Comfort

Someday you will be faced with the reality of loss. And as life goes on, days rolling into nights, it will become clear that you never really stop missing someone special who's gone; you just learn to live around the gaping hole of their absence.

When you lose someone you can't imagine living without, your heart breaks wide open, and the bad news is you never completely get over the loss. You will never forget them. However, in a backwards way, this is also the good news. They will live on in the warmth of your broken heart that doesn't fully heal back up, and you will continue to grow and experience life, even with your wound. It's like badly breaking an ankle that never heals perfectly and that still hurts when you dance, but you dance anyway with a slight limp, and this limp just adds to the depth of your performance and the authenticity of your character. The people you lose remain a part of you. Remember them and always cherish the good moments spent with them.

—Unknown

At some point in life, we all face separation from the people closest to our hearts. It could be our children moving away from home. A part of life, yes, but as excited as we (and they) are for their new adventure, it is accompanied by mixed emotions. Bittersweet. Maybe you are that person moving away from family or friends—excited to go but aware of who you are leaving behind and the memories you will share across the miles.

Ultimately, the people we love leave us through death, the most painful of losses. In grief, we can find comfort in each other. I can't think of a better way to provide that comfort than with a quilt made with a lost loved one's clothes to surround us with warmth and love.

Leaving the Nest Quilt

LINDA + BRENDAN

Linda works in communications and is the mom of Colin (22) and Brendan (19). Brendan is a student at McGill University in Montreal.

Their family has experienced an intense series of changes and emotions, including cancer diagnosis for Linda's second husband, Richard, and, devastatingly, Richard's death in 2013. This quilt is about the inevitable changes that happen in life, and, in spite of hardship, the happy memories and connections that remain.

On remembering

BRENDAN: I remember some of the clothing. Maybe.

Mighty Machine shorts: They're hilarious! I don't remember wearing them, but I was obsessed with Mighty Machines.

Bug shirt: I always liked nature, especially as a kid.

Shirt with fish: This is more recent. I'd spend multiple hours a day in the forest at our cottage.

Moosehead shirt: This is the shirt Richard wore all the time at the cottage.

Badminton shirts and hockey sock: Once I started taking Badminton seriously, I knew I would be playing it for a long time. I quit hockey for it.

About change and letting go

LINDA: Ever since my kids were little, I've kept a lot of clothes. They were just so cute—I couldn't part with them. I keep everything in bins in my basement.

It's hard to let go of the clothes. You think, "What if?" But my kids never wore the clothes from my childhood. You can't always reuse them 20 or 30 years later.

I didn't cry when I brought Brendan to university the first time. So that was good. I cried the week before. It's the end of an era, as dramatic as that sounds. And because my kids and I have had such intense times, you become a solid unit. When someone leaves the unit, it's like, "Wait, what?" But I also know that connection is always going to be strong.

On the legacy of a life well lived

BRENDAN: I think it's interesting to have a memory quilt made. It shows how a lot of things have changed—in the clothes and in your life. You just have to adapt to it.

LINDA: The quilt gives you the chance to relive all those moments and to have something tangible— a day-to-day touch point. Brendan will know his stories and can tell them to his future kids.

It's fundamental to know where you came from—it's your sense of belonging. What I want my kids to know is how much they are valued and loved. I'm hoping the quilt will also come with a lot of laughs, even eye rolling, like, "Oh my god, *Mom*!" And I'll take that, because that is love.

I hope to instill in my kids that our lives are a patch-work of stories. We've had a lot of difficult experi-ences. It's important to look back and remember joy and happiness and good times. Life is hard enough. The quilt is a good reminder to laugh, do the things you love, and help others. To just be happy.

Linda + Brendan: Initial

Finished quilt: 20˝ × 30˝

Materials

Yardages are based on 40˝ usable width, except where noted. Refer to Preparing Clothing for Quilting (page 22) to prepare the clothing fabric listed below before cutting it. Clothing quantities are approximate.

FOR HALF-SQUARE TRIANGLES:

CLOTHING (3 MEDIUM TO DARK COLORS): 3 adult shirts *or* 8–10 baby-size shirts

CLOTHING *or* QUILTING COTTON (LIGHT): 1 adult shirt *or* ⅓ yard

FOR SOLID SQUARES:

CLOTHING *or* QUILTING COTTON (LIGHT AND 3 MEDIUM TO DARK COLORS): 1 adult shirt *or* ⅓ yard

FOR INITIAL:

FABRIC A (LIGHT): ⅛ yard of quilting cotton

FABRIC B (MEDIUM): ½ yard or 1 fat quarter of quilting cotton

FABRIC C (DARK): 1 fat quarter of quilting cotton

> **Fabric:**
> Good for all.

BACKING: ¾ yard

BATTING: 28˝ × 38˝

BINDING: ⅓ yard

FAST2CUT SIMPLE SQUARE TEMPLATES (by C&T Publishing; *optional*)

NONPERMANENT MARKING TOOL, such as a Hera Marker

TEMPLATE MATERIAL, such as Visi-GRID Quilter's Template Sheets (by C&T Publishing), *or* HEAVY CARD STOCK

Cutting

Measure twice + cut once!

HALF-SQUARE TRIANGLES

- Cut 9 squares 6˝ × 6˝ from the medium to dark clothing.
- Cut 9 squares 6˝ × 6˝ from the light clothing or quilting cotton.

SOLID SQUARES

- Cut 7 squares 5½˝ × 5½˝ from clothing or quilting cotton.

INITIAL

Choose a dimensional font from your computer or online, or download the free 3D letters from my website (ateliersixdesign.com/downloads). Make sure to pick a font that you can cut into separate pieces to create a 3D look, using Fabrics A (light/highlight), B (medium/main), and C (dark/shadow).

Enlarge to around 16˝ tall and print, copy, or trace the pieces of your chosen initial onto template material or heavy card stock.

Cut out the template pieces. Place the template (both right sides facing up) and trace on to the light, medium, and dark cotton. For machine appliqué, you do not need to add a seam allowance. For needle-turn appliqué, leave enough space between the pieces to add a narrow seam allowance when cutting.

Piecing

Seam allowances are ¼″ unless otherwise noted. Refer to the quilt assembly diagram (below) as needed.

HALF-SQUARE TRIANGLE BLOCKS

My favorite way to create half-square triangles with clothing is the two-at-a-time method (below). It works well for kids' clothes, where you don't have a lot of surface area to work with.

However, if you are fussy cutting a directional motif or print, use the one-at-a-time method (at right) to cut the squares in half (diagonally) first. This is the easier and safer bet to make sure the motifs are facing the desired direction.

Two-at-a-Time Method

1. With right sides together, pair each 6″ × 6″ medium to dark clothing square with a 6″ × 6″ light clothing / quilting-cotton square.

2. Using a nonpermanent marking tool, trace a diagonal line through the center of the square as shown. Press firmly to make a crease in both layers. Pin together the 2 squares, ensuring all edges align.

3. Sew ¼″ on either side of the marked line as shown.

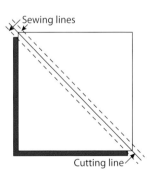

4. Cut the sewn squares in half diagonally along the marked line to make 2 half-square triangles.

5. Press the seams open and trim to 5½″ × 5½″.

One-at-a-Time Method
(for Directional Motifs and Prints)

1. Cut directional motif squares and coordinating squares in half diagonally, taking your desired position into account.

2. With right sides together, sew the diagonal seam.

3. Press the seam open and trim to 5½″ × 5½″.

QUILT TOP ASSEMBLY

1. Arrange the 5½″ × 5½″ half-square triangle and solid square blocks into 6 rows of 4 blocks each.

2. Sew together the blocks into rows. Press the seams open.

3. Sew together the rows, matching vertical seams. Press the seams open.

4. Square and trim the quilt top to 20½″ × 30½″.

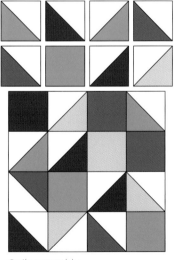

Quilt assembly

Finishing

Layer the quilt top, batting, and backing to make a quilt sandwich. Baste, quilt, and bind using your preferred methods.

Tip: Optional Hanging Sleeve

If you want to display the quilt on a wall, attach a 4″ × 19″ hanging sleeve.

APPLIQUÉ

1. Position the pieces of the initial on the quilt top, being careful to align the different pieces. Baste it into place using your preferred technique.

2. Sew around each piece using needle-turn appliqué *or*, for raw-edge appliqué by machine, using a straight stitch, zigzag stitch, blanket stitch, or other favorite embroidery stitch. Remove the basting stitches or pins.

Comfort Quilt

SONJA, DIANA, ROSA + CLOVELLY

Sonja (49) and her mum, Diana (72), remain close despite living on opposite sides of the world. 11 years ago, Sonja and her Canadian husband, John, moved from Australia to Montreal, where they live with their kids Finley and Clovelly. Sonja and Di cherish their relationship with Di's late mother, Rosa. Their quilt is about the love and comfort of family, 4 generations of maternal lineage, and the invisible umbilical cord that keeps them close.

About leaving home

SONJA: Relocating was a big upheaval. It took one very special man to get me to leave an amazing lifestyle and family. I'm so thankful that my mum comes out every few years. I still, at the age of 49, need my mother! And I miss her like crazy.

DI: Of course I miss Sonja very much.

On remembering …

SONJA: Nan's name was Rosa, and she had a green thumb. Her backyard was big and full of beautiful roses. She had a little birdbath, and all the sparrows would come.

DI: If I could now, I would spend days with her in the garden. Or shopping. She bought beautiful clothes and always looked stunning.

Sonja and Di reminisce while looking through clothing.

... and finding comfort

SONJA: I still miss Nan. And I miss my mum, even though she's still alive—just too far away. The quilt will be my comfort when I'm feeling tender or sad. I can lay it on my lap, think of them, and feel secure.

DI: When my mother died in 2003, I kept her dressing gown because it still had a smell about it. I put it up in the top of the wardrobe, and every year when I bring it down, I think, "I should throw this out." But I can't.

SONJA: The quilt will be a living thing. You remember the times when they wore the clothing. There's more of a thread, a connection—an umbilical cord, in a way.

DI: I appreciate that the quilt will be with Sonja every day.

SONJA: For you, Mum, you're happy to know that we both have a bit of Nan. And I have something of yours that makes me happy. And you like the idea that in the future your history will be ...

DI: ... in the tapestry.

SONJA: Yes. Preserved and passed down. I'll tell many, many stories.

DI: As long as they are true!

SONJA: I'll always tell stories about Mum, Nan, and how much I revere them.

DI: I live for my family. Family is very important. We might fight, but we have each other.

SONJA: I can't express what it's like to feel the love of my mum, grandma, and daughter. For my daughter, it feels like the umbilical cord is always there. Now I realize I have that cord with my mother and my grandmother, and I can pull on it when I need it. We're all connected. Still.

Sonja + Di with Clovelly

Sonja, Diana, Rosa + Clovelly: Otherwise/*Autrement*

Finished quilt: 45″ × 60″

Materials

Yardages are based on 40″ usable width, except where noted. Refer to Preparing Clothing for Quilting (page 22) to prepare the clothing fabric listed below before cutting it. Clothing quantities are approximate.

FABRIC A: 2¼ yards of quilting cotton for background

CLOTHING: 24 pieces of baby clothing (approximately 2–3 strips per item) *or* 12 pieces of kid clothing (approximately 4–5 strips per item) *or* 6 pieces of adult clothing (approximately 8–9 strips per item)

BACKING: 3 yards

BATTING: 53″ × 68″

BINDING: ½ yard

NONPERMANENT MARKING TOOL, such as a Hera Marker

QUILTING RULER WITH 45°-ANGLE MARK

Fabric:
Good for all.

Tip: Designing Your Quilt

It's very helpful to download the coloring sheets (page 16) and map out the color placement for this quilt. You can also photograph your clothing in the order you would like it to appear and use the photo for reference. Also consider sewing clothing pieces together for larger shapes as needed.

Cutting

Refer to Cutting Parallelograms (page 80) to follow the cutting instructions.

Measure twice + cut once!

NOTE | Label As You Cut

Labeling as you cut the pieces is a must for this quilt. I use painter's tape; it's quick and easy. If you don't want to interrupt the flow of cutting, you can premake labels all together or one column at a time.

Cutting continued on page 81

CUTTING PARALLELOGRAMS

Due to the deconstructed chevron design, the parallelograms have opposing angles. Be sure to keep this in mind when using directional prints or fabrics that are not the same on the front and back.

The opposing angles are labeled NW (northwest = the uppermost point of the parallelogram is on the top left) and NE (northeast = the uppermost point of the parallelogram is on the top right), and this matches how they are placed in the quilt.

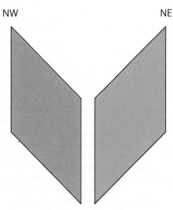

NW   NE

Northwest and northeast

Cutting Guide

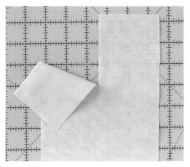

1. Tear or cut the strips as indicated in the cutting charts (next page and pages 82–84).

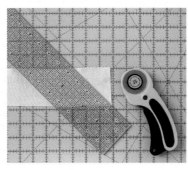

2. Using a ruler with a 45°-angle mark, trim the end at a 45° angle.

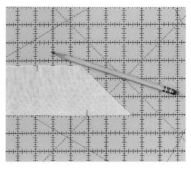

3. Measure the height of the parallelogram you are cutting, as indicated in the cutting charts. Mark each side of the strip.

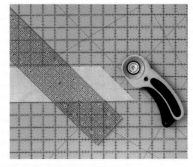

4. Cut the piece at the marks made in Step 3.

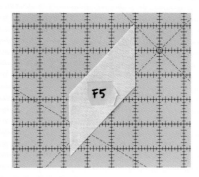

5. Label the piece.

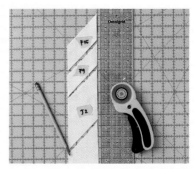

6. Continue cutting the strip into parallelograms with the measurements listed in the cutting charts.

FABRIC A (BACKGROUND)

Refer to the quilt assembly diagram (page 86) as needed. Shaded columns are for reference only.

1. Cut or tear 3 strips 4¼″ × 81″. Subcut as follows.

Strip number	Piece label	Strip width (with seam allowance)	Direction	Qty.	Height (with seam allowance)	Height (finished)
1	E5	4¼″	NW	1	8¼″	7½″
1	E1	4¼″	NW	1	6¾″	6″
1	I2, I6, I8, I10	4¼″	NW	4	6¼″	5½″
1	E3, E9, E11, I4	4¼″	NW	4	5½″	4¾″
1	E7	4¼″	NW	1	2¼″	1½″
2	I12	4¼″	NW	1	4½″	3¾″
2	B6	4¼″	NE	1	5½″	4¾″
2	B2, D8	4¼″	NE	2	4½″	3¾″
2	D2, D4, D10, D12	4¼″	NE	4	3½″	2¾″
2	B4, B8	4¼″	NE	2	3¼″	2½″
2	D6	4¼″	NE	1	2½″	1¾″
2	B11	4¼″	Rectangle	1	28″	27¾″
3	E14	4¼″	Rectangle	1	18¼″	18″
3	C12	2¾″ (Trim the 4¼″ strip.)	Rectangle	1	26″	25¾″
3	J5	2¾″ (Trim the 4¼″ strip.)	Rectangle	1	23¼″	23″

Tip: Cutting Order for Clothing

It's easiest to cut the pieces in order by column, labeling each piece. To keep things organized, use the coloring sheet or photo guide (see Designing Your Quilt, page 78), checking clothing pieces off as you cut. Using a design wall (see Design Wall, page 23) is very helpful when cutting this quilt.

2. Cut or tear 3 strips 2¾″ × 81″. Subcut as follows.

Strip number	Piece label	Strip width (with seam allowance)	Direction	Qty.	Height (with seam allowance)	Height (finished)
1	G1	2¾″	NW	1	11″	10¼
1	G9	2¾″	NW	1	10¾″	10″
1	C7	2¾″	NW	1	9″	8¼″
1	G5	2¾″	NW	1	6¾″	6″
1	C5, C9, G3	2¾″	NW	3	5″	4¼″
1	C1, C3, G11	2¾″	NW	3	4½″	3¾″
1	G7	2¾″	NW	1	3½″	2¾″
2	J2	2¾″	NE	1	4½″	3¾″
2	F1, F11, H2, H4, H8, H10	2¾″	NE	6	3½″	2¾″
2	F3, F7, F13, F17, H6	2¾″	NE	5	2¾″	2″
2	F9	2¾″	NE	1	2″	1¼″
2	F5, F15	2¾″	NE	2	2¼″	1½″
2	G14	2¾″	Rectangle	1	8¾″	8½″
2	F20	2¾″	Rectangle	1	4¼″	4″
3	K	2¾″	Rectangle	1	60½″	60½″

3. For Column A, cut 1 rectangle 60″ × 17″. From the remaining 17″ × 21″ strip, subcut:

Strip number	Piece label	Strip width (with seam allowance)	Direction	Qty.	Height (with seam allowance)	Height (finished)
1	B10, D14, E13, I14	4¾″	Squares; subcut each into 2 half-square triangles.	2	4¾″	3¾″
1	C11, F19, G13, J4	3¼″	Squares; subcut each into 2 half-square triangles.	2	3¼″	2¼″
1	I15	4¼″	Rectangle	1	8¾″	8½″
1	D15	4¼″	Rectangle	1	8¼″	8″

CLOTHING

Refer to the quilt assembly diagram (page 86) as needed. Shaded columns are for reference only.

Cut the following pieces from the clothing.

Piece label	Strip width (with seam allowance)	Direction	Qty.	Height (with seam allowance)	Height (finished)
B1	4¼″	NE	1	3¼″	2½″
B3	4¼″	NE	1	4½″	3¾″
B5	4¼″	NE	1	5½″	4¾″
B7	4¼″	NE	1	6¼″	5½″
B9	4¼″	NE	1	3¼″	2½″
C2	2¾″	NW	1	2¾″	2″
C4	2¾″	NW	1	2¼″	1½″
C6	2¾″	NW	1	3¾″	3″
C8	2¾″	NW	1	2¼″	1½″
C10	2¾″	NW	1	2¾″	2″
D1	4¼″	NE	1	4¾″	4″
D3	4¼″	NE	1	6¾″	6″
D5	4¼″	NE	1	5½″	4¾″
D7	4¼″	NE	1	6¾″	6″
D9	4¼″	NE	1	6¼″	5½″
D11	4¼″	NE	1	6¼″	5½″
D13	4¼″	NE	1	5½″	4¾″
E2	4¼″	NW	1	2″	1¼″
E4	4¼″	NW	1	3¼″	2½″
E6	4¼″	NW	1	2″	1¼″
E8	4¼″	NW	1	4½″	3¾″
E10	4¼″	NW	1	2″	1¼″
E12	4¼″	NW	1	3¼″	2½″
F2	2¾″	NE	1	5¾″	5″
F4	2¾″	NE	1	3¾″	3″
F6	2¾″	NE	1	5¾″	5″

Chart continued on page 84

Piece label	Strip width (with seam allowance)	Direction	Qty.	Height (with seam allowance)	Height (finished)
F8	2¾″	NE	1	6¾″	6″
F10	2¾″	NE	1	5¾″	5″
F12	2¾″	NE	1	5¾″	5″
F14	2¾″	NE	1	3¾″	3″
F16	2¾″	NE	1	5¾″	5″
F18	2¾″	NE	1	2¾″	2″
G2	2¾″	NW	1	2¾″	2″
G4	2¾″	NW	1	3¾″	3″
G6	2¾″	NW	1	2¼″	1½″
G8	2¾″	NW	1	3¾″	3″
G10	2¾″	NW	1	2¾″	2″
G12	2¾″	NW	1	3¾″	3″
H1	2¾″	NE	1	4¾″	4″
H3	2¾″	NE	1	5¾″	5″
H5	2¾″	NE	1	12½″	11¾″
H7	2¾″	NE	1	5¾″	5″
H9	2¾″	NE	1	5¾″	5″
H11	2¾″	NE	1	18¼″	17½″
I1	4¼″	NW	1	4½″	3¾″
I3	4¼″	NW	1	4½″	3¾″
I5	4¼″	NW	1	3¼″	2½″
I7	4¼″	NW	1	2″	1¼″
I9	4¼″	NW	1	3¼″	2½″
I11	4¼″	NW	1	5½″	4¾″
I13	4¼″	NW	1	3¼″	2½″
J1	2¾″	NE	1	22¼″	21½″
J3	2¾″	NE	1	12½″	11¾″

Piecing

Seam allowances are ¼″ unless otherwise noted. Refer to the quilt assembly diagram (page 86) as needed.

1. With right sides together, sew together the parallelogram, half-square triangle, and rectangle pieces for Column B, referring to the quilt assembly diagram for placement. Press all seams open, being careful to keep the sides of the pieced strip straight.**(A)**

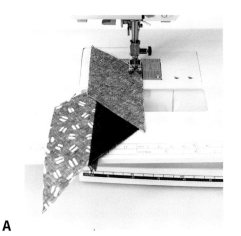

A

Tip: Piecing Bias Seams

When sewing together bias seams, I try to place the less stretchy fabric on top. Along with the machine's feed dogs, this helps to control the stretchier fabric on bottom. In this quilt, sometimes the less stretchy piece will be the starched clothing and sometimes the quilting cotton.

If any bias seams accidentally stretch while sewing, carefully press them with steam to correct a small amount of stretch and help realign the piece.

2. Strip piece Columns C–J together in the same manner as in Step 1, referring to the quilt assembly diagram for each column. Press the seams open.

3. Starting at the bottom flat edge, trim and square all wide pieced strips to 4¼″ wide and all narrow pieced strips to 2¾″ wide.

4. For Column H, trim the bottom (piece H11) 2¼″ up from the bottommost point (SW point on the bottom left). Continue to trim Column H in the same manner as in Step 3. **(B)**

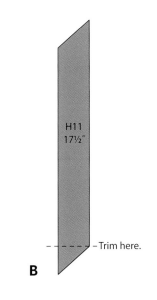

H11
17½″

– – – Trim here.

B

Tip: Squaring the Pieced Strips

If the piecing in the strips is slightly off in a few spots and the sides are not aligned, it is preferable to trim the columns so that they are square rather than trying to achieve the desired width. Because the chevron points are offset, it will not affect the piecing of the columns together.

5. Pin and sew together 2 columns at a time, as shown: B/C, D/E, F/G, H/I, and J/K. Press the seams open. **(C)**

6. Pin and sew together the combined strips from Step 5. Press the seams open. Press the parallelogram panel.

7. Pin and sew Strip A to the parallelogram panel as shown in the quilt assembly diagram (page 86). Press the seams open.

8. Square and trim the quilt top to 45½″ × 60½″.

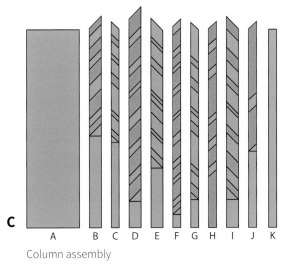

C

A   B   C   D   E   F   G   H   I   J   K

Column assembly

Finishing

Layer the quilt top, batting, and backing to make a quilt sandwich. Baste, quilt, and bind using your preferred methods.

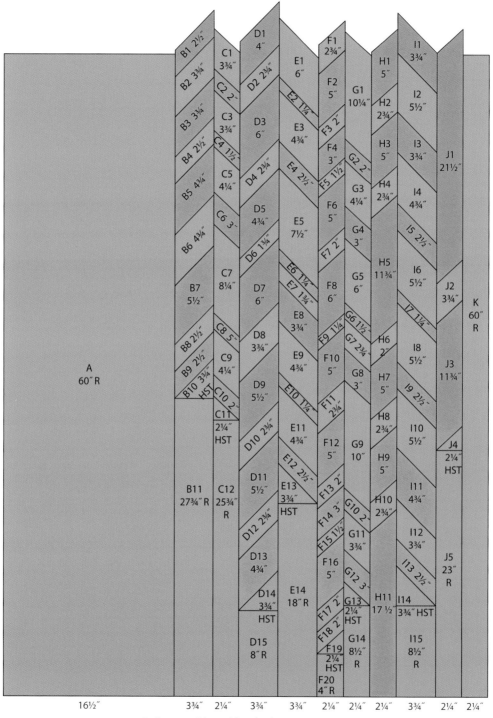

Quilt assembly and finished measurements

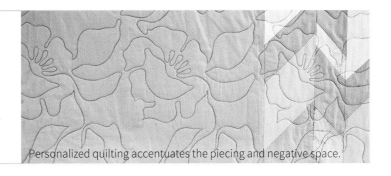

Personalized quilting accentuates the piecing and negative space.

Healing and Connection Quilt

SOPHIE, BEAR + SIMON

Canadian Sophie and her son, Simon, live in Australia—a move made in part to be closer to family. In 2014, Sophie's husband and Simon's dad, Andrew ("Bear"), passed away from melanoma, a cancer he had been fighting for two years while Sophie was undergoing treatment for breast cancer.

When Sophie received the first memory quilt I made for her from Andrew's clothes, I received this note:

"I loved pointing out all the pieces to Simon and explaining where they came from, and he even remembered some of them! ('Oh, Daddy used to wear this red shirt all the time!') Which is great, because at times he is upset about not remembering him too well … "

This statement about how the death of a parent impacts children moved me deeply. The quilt featured in this book is just for Simon—to help him stay connected to his dad.

Simon and his dad on his parents' wedding day

Photos from the Bourguignon-Rich family's collection

About Andrew

We met on the internet, completely by chance. Within a few days we were writing to each other every day, then talking twice a day. He moved to Canada within a year and we had a beautiful son together.

Andrew was the love of my life, my best friend, and the world's greatest and most loving daddy. Bear loved life like no other, and he had a great sense of humor. I miss hearing him laugh.

About the grieving process

I did not clean out his side of the closet or his dresser for two years. It was only when we started to move to Australia that I realized it would not make sense to take his clothes with us.

His clothes were such a part of how I pictured him that it was really hard to think about letting them go or even cutting them up. Not only is the quilt a unique way to give the clothes a new purpose, but it also helped me let go of the material *stuff* while honoring the memories attached to the individual pieces of clothing. The quilt makes it feel like he is still close.

I love that his Simpsons flannel pajamas and a cap with a joke on it were used. Memory quilts cannot honor our loved ones properly if they make us sad. They have to make us smile, if not laugh.

Photo by Suzanne Paquette

Sophie's first memory quilt, made with Andrew's clothes and inspired by Rainbow Beach

Photo by Sophie Bourguignon

Bear in his red shirt

Sophie's wishes for Simon

I want our son to understand that his daddy was a real person and that he was part of our daily lives. He was *here*. If God gave us an hour together, I would gladly let Simon have 50 minutes of it and keep only 10 for myself.

A quilt is so much more tangible than photographs. It makes the memories more "real." It was of the utmost importance that I find a way to make those memories come alive.

Sophie, Bear + Simon: Connect the Dots

Finished quilt: 40˝ × 50˝

Materials

Yardages are based on 40˝ usable width, except where noted. Refer to Preparing Clothing for Quilting (page 22) to prepare the clothing fabric listed below before cutting it. Clothing quantities are approximate.

Quilting-cotton yardage amounts listed are the maximum quantities you need (that is, the amount needed to make the quilt solely in quilting cotton). Depending on how much clothing you use, your cotton requirements will vary but will not be higher than the yardage listed.

Fabric: Good for all. Thick fabric friendly. Best for clothing that can accommodate 10½˝ × 10½˝ squares.

QUILTING COTTON:

FABRIC A (LIGHT NEUTRAL): ⅝ yard

FABRIC B (MEDIUM NEUTRAL): ⅓ yard or 1 fat quarter

FABRIC C (DARK NEUTRAL): ⅓ yard or 1 fat quarter

FABRIC D (LIGHT MAIN): ⅝ yard

FABRIC E (MEDIUM MAIN): 1 yard

FABRIC F (DARK MAIN): ⅓ yard

FABRIC G (MEDIUM CONTRAST): ⅓ yard or 1 fat quarter

FABRIC H (DARK CONTRAST): ⅓ yard or 1 fat quarter

or

CLOTHING: 24 pieces of baby clothing *or* 12 pieces of kid clothing *or* 8 pieces of adult clothing to fulfill the colors specified

GROUND FABRIC: Scraps of clothing and/or fabric for reverse-appliqué patina

BACKING: 2¾ yards

BATTING: 48˝ × 58˝

BINDING: ½ yard

NOTE | Clothing + Fabric Selection

To achieve the overall balance of value in this design, the colors are divided into three different groups (neutral, main, and contrast) with different values within each group (light, medium, and dark). Sorting the clothing by these groupings can help you plan the quilt design and also give you hints of where you may want to add quilting cotton to pull everything together.

Fabrics within a particular group and value need not be all the same. As long as they have the overall feeling of the same color and the same value, you will achieve the desired result. If you aren't sure, squint your eyes when looking at each group. Any pieces that are too different from the overall feeling of the group will stand out.

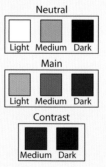

Color groupings segmented by value

Same color groupings in fabric

Cutting

Using the convex circle and concave circle patterns (pullout page P1), trace and cut templates from template material. Note: *For the concave pattern, tape two sheets of template material together to make the template.*

Measure twice + cut once!

FABRIC A OR CLOTHING:
1 square 10½″ × 10½″
and 9 squares 6¾″ × 6¾″

FABRIC B OR CLOTHING:
1 square 10½″ × 10½″
and 1 square 6¾″ × 6¾″

FABRIC C OR CLOTHING:
1 square 10½″ × 10½″
and 2 squares 6¾″ × 6¾″

FABRIC D OR CLOTHING:
4 squares 10½″ × 10½″

FABRIC E OR CLOTHING:
6 squares 10½″ × 10½″
and 3 squares 6¾″ × 6¾″

FABRIC F OR CLOTHING:
3 squares 10½″ × 10½″

FABRIC G OR CLOTHING:
1 square 10½″ × 10½″

FABRIC H OR CLOTHING:
3 squares 10½″ × 10½″

OPTIONAL TECHNIQUE: CREATING *a* PATINA EFFECT

Since this quilt features easy piecing of simple, same-size blocks, I wanted to add an extra textural dimension to the blocks, soften the clean edges that the piecing creates, and add an improvised feeling.

A patina effect is created by randomly cutting jagged holes, reverse raw-edge appliquéing, and machine embroidering. The quarter-circles are then set in and, if needed, a bit more machine embroidery can be added on top.

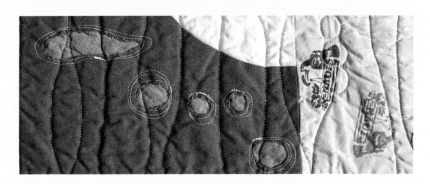

Note: Using a stronger starch helps the blocks keep their shape if you are doing a lot of machine embroidery.

1. Select the 10½″ × 10½″ squares that you would like to patina. Using sharp shears, randomly cut out small irregular, jagged holes. You can also cut corners, strips, or any shape you like. The parts you cut out will be filled in with your chosen ground fabric.

2. Place pieces of your chosen ground fabric underneath the cut holes, ensuring they are at least ¼″ larger than the perimeter of the hole.

Alternatively, you can cut a 10½″ × 10½″ square from the ground fabric and place it under the top fabric. This works well when you have made several holes. Pin or glue baste together the ground and top fabrics.

3. With the right side facing up, edgestitch around the perimeter of the holes, approximately ⅛″ from the edge of the hole.

4. Turn over the block and trim the excess ground fabric, leaving an approximate ¼″ seam allowance around each hole.

5. With the right side facing up, machine embroider the block in the desired pattern. Using a variegated thread helps create a painterly look.

QUARTER-CIRCLES

1. Using the convex circle template, cut out quarter-circles from the 6¾″ × 6¾″ blocks.

2. Referring to the quilt assembly diagram (page 94), determine the layout and orientation of the 10½″ × 10½″ squares.

3. Pair the quarter-circles to the squares in Step 2.

4. Using the concave circle template, cut out the quarter-circles from the squares in Step 2. Labeling each piece with painter's tape or using a design wall will help you keep track as you go.

Piecing

Seam allowances are ¼″ unless otherwise noted. Refer to the quilt assembly diagram (page 94) as needed.

QUARTER-CIRCLE BLOCKS

1. With right sides together, pin and sew the convex curves to their coordinating square blocks with concave curves.

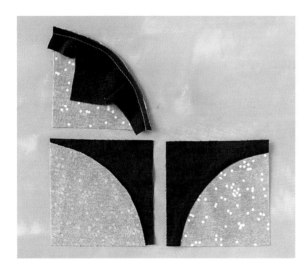

2. Press the seams away from the quarter-circle inset, and trim the blocks to 10½″ × 10½″.

SEWING CURVES

As a milliner, I have sewn a lot of curves in a lot of different fabrics. A few tricks help create a smoother, pucker-free curve that is quick and easy to sew.

On a medium-size curve (like the one in this quilt), I tend to pin in three places: beginning, middle, and end, with the pin perpendicular to the seam edge. (This prevents slipping, which can happen if the pin is placed parallel to the seam edge.) If this doesn't feel controlled enough, add two more pins at the midpoints between the middle and ends.

I usually sew with the concave curve on the bottom and the convex curve on the top. The feed dogs help ease in the concave curve, which tends to stretch more than the convex. It's also easier to keep the edges aligned with the concave curve.

An exception is if the convex curve is made out of a stretchier fabric than the concave one. In this case, I sew with the concave, less stretchy fabric on top or starch the stretchier convex piece more so that it behaves like a woven fabric.

In general, I find that the fabric tells me what it wants to do. When I listen to that, things work out the best.

BLOCK ASSEMBLY

1. Arrange the blocks in 5 rows of 4 blocks each. Move or rotate the blocks as desired to achieve your preferred layout.

Tip: Auditioning Different Layouts

Taking photos of different layout variations lets me compare them, and if I undo a layout that I end up deciding was the best version, I have a reference to go back to. Viewing a design through a camera lens also provides a different perspective; I find this helps me choose the best variation.

2. Sew together the blocks in each row. Press the seams open. If you do not have a photo reference of your layout, be sure to label the pieces or pin them together as you take them off the design wall.

3. Sew together each row, being careful to align the vertical seams. Press the seams open.

Quilt assembly

Finishing

Layer the quilt top, batting, and backing to make a quilt sandwich. Baste, quilt, and bind using your preferred methods.

Personalization: *Appliqué*

To add a symbol of Simon's native country and the place where he lived with his dad, I improv pieced scraps of his dad's clothing, cut a maple leaf shape, and raw-edge appliquéd it to the quilt top after quilting.

A memento of Simon's Canadian heritage

Kindred Pillows, 8 Variations

LOIS + FAMILY

When my grannie, Lois Evelyn Boone McClelland Wilson, was turning 88, the family decided to put together a book of memories for her as a gift to reminisce about family memories and the old house. My mom and her siblings, and their spouses and kids, all jotted down a few reflections about "The House That Grannie Built."

My grandmother passed away at the age of 96 a few years ago, and I am more grateful than ever to have this documentation of stories about her and the family home in Cantley, Quebec. (The excerpt here was written by my mom and my aunt Joan.) These memories, as well as her beloved fur coat, were the inspiration for the modern heirloom pillows.

Lois in her fur coat

The house that Grannie built

Constructed around the turn of the century, "The House that Grannie Built" was originally the United Church manse, a house for the minister and his family. In 1946, Cantley, Quebec natives Lois and Harold moved their young family from Ottawa back to the small village where they had grown up and gotten married. Joan was seven, Sandra was four, and Grant was just a baby.

The house had no working plumbing or electricity for the first six months. There was a summer kitchen and back stairs that exited near the bathroom. Baths were taken in the claw-foot tub, with the water heated downstairs in the kitchen and carried upstairs in pails. Quite a shock for city kids!

Photo from the McClelland family's collection

Grannie Lois's house in Cantley, Quebec

The basement, which needed vast repairs, once held an enormous wood furnace in it that took 4′-long pieces of wood into its grate, three or four at a time. The floor of the basement was always covered in bark that had fallen off from the stored firewood, which had been chucked through the cellar window after cutting.

The family would call this home for three short years before Harold died, leaving the house habitable and debt-free to a young mother of three.

Lois married Neil Wilson in 1958. Soon the grandchildren arrived, and Lois began looking forward to visits from the extended family. When all fifteen family members were together, the house was alive with laughter and the smell of something good cooking in the kitchen.

Grant, Joan, Sandra, and Lois (Grannie)

Although the McClelland-Wilson property was sold, the house remains recognizable and symbolizes the emergence of a family of two generations from Lois Evelyn Boone McClelland Wilson.

Me in my grannie's fur coat

My grannie's fur coat

When my grandmother passed away, I knew I wanted to save her fur coat. Imbued in the hairs of the fur are memories of winter and Christmas at her house and the smell of her perfume—happy memories. Even her signature piece of tissue in the pocket was still there when I went to deconstruct the coat!

I really wanted to capture the mixture of bucolic farm life that is part of our family's history and the strong, dignified, and fashionable working woman that my grandmother was. And now each of us will have something tangible to remember her and our favorite family stories.

Lois + family:
Striped Half-Square Triangle Pillows

Finished pillows: 18″ × 18″ each

Materials

Yardages are based on 40″ usable width, except where noted. Refer to Preparing Clothing for Quilting (page 22) to prepare the clothing fabric listed below before cutting it. Clothing quantities are approximate.

Fabric:
Good for all.

NOTE | Mix and Match

Making two Lois blocks gives you two finished pillow fronts 18″ × 18″ or a front and back for one pillow. I like to have wholecloth backs on pillows so that I can have two looks and can change my decor with the flip of a pillow.

For *both* pillows in each set

Note: The fabric amounts are for both pillows in the set. Fur was substituted in for some of the dark gray cotton in each of the pillow sets.

PILLOWS 1 + 1A

   FABRIC A (DARK GRAY): ½ yard

   FABRIC B (WHITE): ⅛ yard

   FABRIC C (DARK ORANGE): ¼ yard

PILLOWS 2 + 2A

   FABRIC A (DARK GRAY): ⅜ yard

   FABRIC D (PINK): ⅜ yard

   FABRIC E (LIGHT ORANGE): ¼ yard

PILLOWS 3 + 3A

   FABRIC A (DARK GRAY): ⅜ yard

   FABRIC B (WHITE): ⅜ yard

   FABRIC C (DARK ORANGE): ¼ yard

PILLOWS 4 + 4A

   FABRIC A (DARK GRAY): ⅜ yard

   FABRIC D (PINK): ⅜ yard

   FABRIC E (LIGHT ORANGE): ¼ yard

EACH PAIR OF PILLOWS

   PILLOW BACK FABRIC: ⅝ yard

   QUILTING COTTON: ⅝ yard to back quilted front of pillow

   BATTING: 21″ × 21″

   ZIPPERS (14″ LONG): 2

   PILLOW INSERTS (18″ × 18″): 2

   NONPERMANENT MARKING TOOL, such as a Hera Marker

   POINTED TOOL, such as Alex Anderson's 4-in-1 Essential Sewing Tool (by C&T Publishing)

Tip: Fabric Selection

For these blocks, I find two contrasting fabrics/clothing pieces (light and dark, patterned and solid, and so on) provide the most interesting results. You can also play with texture, like I did with my grannie's fur coat.

Cutting

Refer to the Lois block variations (pages 101–104) to select the blocks you will make.

Measure twice + cut once!

NOTE | Cutting Strips

My preferred method of cutting strips of woven 100% cotton is to rip the fabric. Ripping keeps the strips—especially long strips—perfectly straight and on grain.

There is a caveat, though, for 100% cotton printed with straight lines. If the straight lines are not printed on grain, the print will appear crooked after ripping. For these fabrics, I almost always cut strips with a rotary cutter and align the strip with the print instead of the grain of the fabric.

LOIS BLOCK VARIATIONS

For the pillows, you combine 2 Striped blocks (pages 101–104) together to make Lois block half-square triangle variations. There are many more combinations to play around with that aren't pictured. See what you can come up with! Lois block variations can also be mixed and matched as desired to create a quilt top layout.

To create the block variations shown, first cut the appropriate pieces for the corresponding Striped blocks.

FOR STRIPED BLOCK 1, CUT:

- 1 strip 5¾″ × 19½″ in Fabric A
- 1 strip 1½″ × 19½″ in Fabric A
- 1 strip 8½″ × 19½″ in Fabric A
- 1 strip 3¼″ × 19½″ in Fabric B
- 1 strip 4″ × 19½″ in Fabric B

FOR STRIPED BLOCK 1A, CUT:

- 1 strip 3¼″ × 19½″ in Fabric A
- 1 strip 4″ × 19½″ in Fabric A
- 1 strip 5¾″ × 19½″ in Fabric B
- 1 strip 1½″ × 19½″ in Fabric B
- 1 strip 8½″ × 19½″ in Fabric B

FOR STRIPED BLOCK 2, CUT:

- 1 strip 4¾″ × 19½″ in Fabric C
- 1 strip 5½″ × 19½″ in Fabric C
- 2 strips 1½″ × 19½″ in Fabric C
- 3 strips 1½″ × 19½″ in Fabric A
- 1 strip 6¾″ × 19½″ in Fabric A

FOR STRIPED BLOCK 2A, CUT:

- 1 strip 4¾″ × 19½″ in Fabric A
- 1 strip 5½″ × 19½″ in Fabric A
- 2 strips 1½″ × 19½″ in Fabric A
- 3 strips 1½″ × 19½″ in Fabric C
- 1 strip 6¾″ × 19½″ in Fabric C

FOR STRIPED BLOCK 3, CUT:

- 1 strip 11¾″ × 19½″ in Fabric D
- 1 strip 8¾″ × 19½″ in Fabric D
- 1 strip 1½″ × 19½″ in Fabric A

FOR STRIPED BLOCK 4, CUT:

- 1 strip 4¾″ × 19½″ in Fabric E
- 1 strip 1½″ × 19½″ in Fabric E
- 1 strip 11¾″ × 19½″ in Fabric A
- 1 strip 4½″ × 19½″ in Fabric A

FOR EACH PILLOW, CUT:

- 1 square 19½″ × 19½″ from pillow top backing fabric
- 1 square 18½″ × 18½″ from pillow back fabric
- 1 square 20″ × 20″ from batting

Piecing

Seam allowances are ¼″ unless otherwise noted.

STRIPED BLOCKS

1. With right sides together, sew strips of contrasting fabric as shown in the Striped block diagrams in Sewing the Lois Blocks (below) for your desired blocks.

2. Press the seams open and trim the blocks to 19½″ × 19½″.

LOIS BLOCKS

Use the Striped blocks to make Lois half-square triangle blocks, referring to the following diagrams to ensure proper right-sides-together placement of the Striped blocks. It is important to place them as shown, or you will get a different result.

Sewing the Lois Blocks

LOIS 1 + 1A

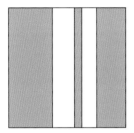

Striped block 1

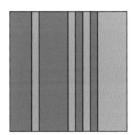

Striped block 2

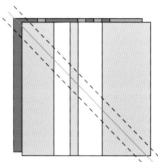

Place right sides together.

Lois pillow 1: Striped blocks 1 & 2

Lois pillow 1A: Striped blocks 1 & 2

LOIS 2 + 2A

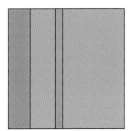

Striped block 4

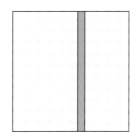

Striped block 3

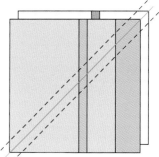

Place right sides together.

Lois pillow 2: Striped blocks 3 & 4

Lois pillow 2A: Striped blocks 3 & 4

LOIS 3 + 3A

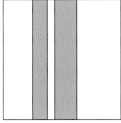

Striped block 1A

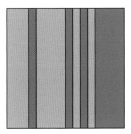

Striped block 2A

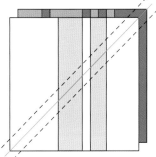

Place right sides together.

Lois pillow 3: Striped blocks 1A & 2A

Lois pillow 3A: Striped blocks 1A & 2A

LOIS 4 + 4A

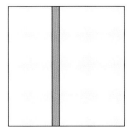

Striped block 3

Striped block 4

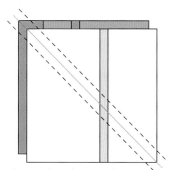

Place right sides together.

Lois pillow 4: Striped blocks 3 & 4

Lois pillow 4A: Striped blocks 3 & 4

1. Place the Striped Blocks right sides together, being careful to align the stripes as shown in the diagrams (pages 101–103 and above).

2. Pin together the blocks. Using a nonpermanent marking tool, mark a line from corner to corner as shown in blue. This will be the cutting line.

3. Stitch ¼″ on either side of the cutting line.

4. Open up the blocks along each stitching line to verify that the stripes are properly aligned.

5. With the 2 blocks lying flat, cut along the cutting line with a rotary cutter to make 2 pillow fronts. Press the seams open. Trim the blocks to 19″ × 19″.

Quilting

Make a quilt sandwich with the pieced pillow front, batting, and pillow top backing. Baste and quilt using your preferred methods. Trim the pillow fronts to 18½″ × 18½″.

Finishing

1. With the zipper right sides together with the pillow top, align the zipper edge along the top pillow edge. Pin the closed zipper to the pillow top and stitch using a zipper foot, starting about ¼˝ before the zipper stopper and ending just after the zipper stopper at the other end. Be sure not to sew all the way from one end of the zipper to the other.

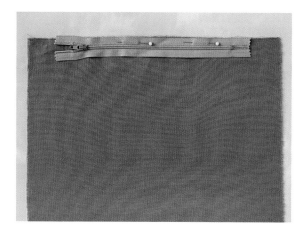
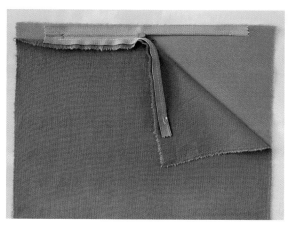

2. Place the zipper right sides together with the pillow back, being careful to align the sides of the pillow pieces. Pin the zipper in place on this side and stitch as indicated in Step 1. Press the seams so that they butt up against each other, concealing the zipper.

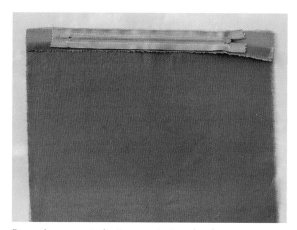
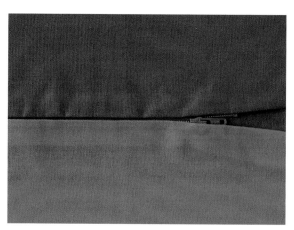

Press the seams to butt up against each other.

3. Slide the zipper halfway open, and fold the pillow top and back right sides together. Stitch with a ½˝ seam around the pillow, being careful to start and stop stitching ¼˝ to the insides of the zipper stoppers.

4. Flip the pillow inside out and use a turning tool to gently push out the corners of the pillow sham.

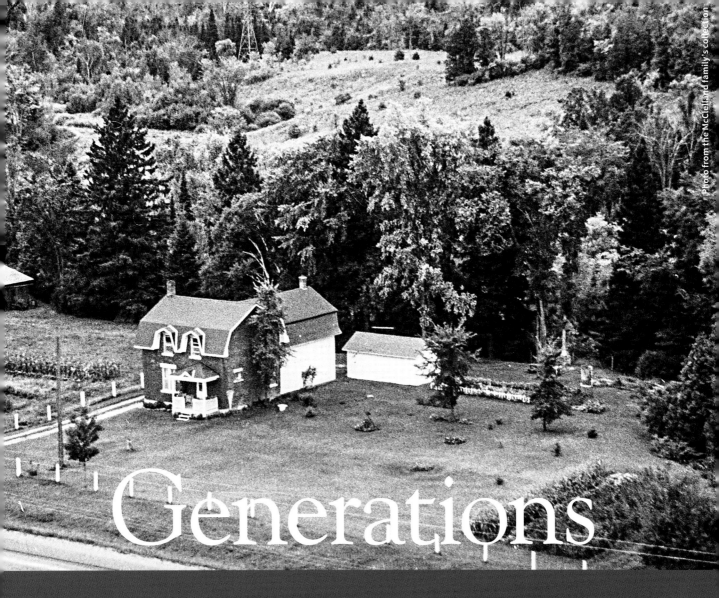

Generations

… the secret of the Great Stories is that they have no secrets. The Great Stories are the ones you have heard and want to hear again. The ones you can enter anywhere and inhabit comfortably. They don't deceive you with thrills and trick endings. They don't surprise you with the unforeseen. They are as familiar as the house you live in. Or the smell of your lover's skin. You know how they end, yet you listen as though you don't. In the way that although you know that one day you will die, you live as though you won't. In the Great Stories you know who lives, who dies, who finds love, who doesn't. And yet you want to know again.

That is their mystery and their magic.

—Arundhati Roy,
The God of Small Things

Family Apron

ANNA, KALEB, OPAL + SOLOMON

Ottawa native Anna is a PhD candidate in Information Science and a university administrator. She and her husband, Kaleb (born in California, raised in Idaho); daughter, Opal; and son, Solomon, loaded everything into a large conversion van in 2013 to make the trek from Seattle to Montreal, where they now live. This apron tells the story of their family.

About growing a family ... and individuals

Kaleb and I met in Seattle. Soon after we met, I was pregnant with Opal. And two years later I had Solomon.

Without family or friends close by, Opal and I spent a lot of time alone together when she was born, just looking at each other and both being totally content. In those moments, I realized she was a little person, not just a baby.

When Solomon was really young, it was hard. We had evolved as a family, and I felt like I never had enough time with him. I missed him so much when I had to go back to work. It's a bittersweet memory.

Opal and Solomon are little perfect people who also make me crazy! I love that they are independent, like us. We all seem to have little bits of each other in ourselves. We're a family and we love each other.

Anna + Kaleb

On sewing and artistic legacy

Kaleb and his whole family sew and are really creative. I don't know if we'd have had enough for this project if it weren't for them. In the apron, there's a piece of a pair of jeans that Kaleb made for me when we were first dating. There are some embroidered linen napkins from my family, too.

I really respect people who sew or knit (like my grandparents). I think it is a great art that should be preserved. Preserving some of my family's work in another work seems very appropriate.

Photo by Suzanne Paquette

About the keeping of things ...

We are a family that doesn't have storage space, and I can't keep much. I'll probably put on the apron once, then hang it up somewhere, keep it safe, and show it off. I want it to last as long as possible. It's a keepsake to look at and hand down.

On recalling memories

Objects or pictures help me recall things, like magic—the memory comes back like yesterday. I value keepsakes: They really are links to the past for me. I do think that if these things disappeared, my memories would float away.

I want the kids to remember where they came from, their friends, and their family. And that I kept these things because I respect them as individuals.

Anna, Kaleb, Opal + Solomon: Onward

Finished apron (without ties): 30″ × 24¾″

Materials

Yardages are based on 40″ usable width, except where noted. Refer to Preparing Clothing for Quilting (page 22) to prepare the clothing fabric listed below before cutting it. Note: For this project, it is recommended to stabilize the clothing with fusible interfacing. Clothing quantities are approximate.

Fabric: Good for most. Thick fabrics are challenging at points and seam intersections.

CLOTHING (OR A MIX OF CLOTHING AND QUILTING COTTON):
37 rectangles 5¾″ × 3¼″ for apron front

FABRIC A (QUILTING COTTON): ⅜ yard for apron front

BACKING: ¾ yard for apron back

LIGHTWEIGHT FUSIBLE INTERFACING (SUCH AS STABILI-TEE FUSIBLE INTERFACING BY C&T PUBLISHING): ⅝ yard or enough to fuse the clothing rectangles

APRON TIES: ¼ yard

NONPERMANENT MARKING TOOL, such as a Hera Marker

LOOP TURNER (*optional*)

TEMPLATE MATERIAL, such as Visi-GRID Quilter's Template Sheets (by C&T Publishing)

Cutting

Using the HRT cutting pattern (pullout page P2), trace and cut templates from template material.

Measure twice + cut once!

FROM THE CLOTHING, CUT:

• 42 rectangles 5¾″ × 3¼″

FROM THE APRON TIE FABRIC, CUT:

• 2 strips 3″ × WOF

FROM FABRIC A, CUT:

• 1 strip 3¼″ × width of fabric. Subcut into:
  6 rectangles 5¾″ × 3¼″

• 1 strip 5½″ × width of fabric. Subcut into:
  1 rectangle 5½″ × 14″
  2 rectangles 5½″ × 9½″
  2 rectangles 5½″ × 5″

Piecing

Seam allowances are ¼˝ unless otherwise noted. Refer to the apron assembly diagram (page 115) as needed.

PREPARING *the* BLOCKS

There are 24 NE-facing half-rectangle triangles (the diagonal starts on the top right) **(A)** and 24 NW-facing half-rectangle triangles (the diagonal starts on the top left) **(B)**. The direction of the half-rectangle triangle is important in cutting and sewing.

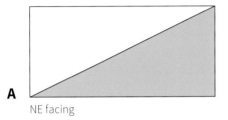

A
NE facing

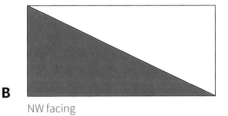

B
NW facing

NOTE | Upper Left Triangle

For the upper left triangle in the large Fabric A triangle, create two pairs of rectangles with the same clothing fabric and Fabric A—one pointing NE and one pointing NW.

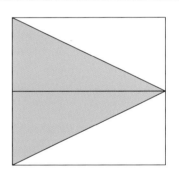

---

1. Match up 36 clothing rectangles to make 18 pairings. The 6 Fabric A rectangles 5¾˝ × 3¼˝ should be each paired with the remaining 6 clothing rectangles. These become the half-rectangle triangles that can be used to make the edges of the large Fabric A triangle in the quilt.

2. Divide the pairings into 2 piles of half-rectangle triangles: NE-pointing and NW-pointing. 3 of the Fabric A / clothing rectangle pairings should be in each pile. If you are planning specific placement for some of the clothing, be mindful of whether it should be in a NE-pointing or NW-pointing half-rectangle triangle.

3. Start with the NE-pointing group of paired rectangles. Place one rectangle right side up and one rectangle wrong side up. On the wrong-side-up rectangle, use a nonpermanent marking tool to mark a dot ½″ from both the upper left and bottom right corners. On the right-side-up rectangle, use a nonpermanent marking tool to mark a dot ½″ from both the lower left and upper right corners.

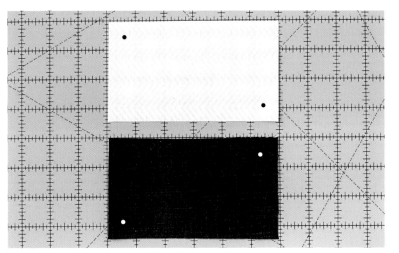

NE-pointing half-rectangle triangle dot placement

4. Draw a line through the dots on both pieces. Place both pieces right sides together and pin together, being sure to align the dots. Mark each pair of NE-pointing rectangles in this same manner.

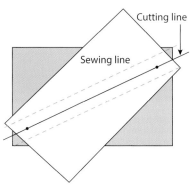

NE sewing + cutting

5. Mark the NW-pointing group of paired rectangles with the same process as Step 3, but placing the dots in the opposite locations. On the right-side-up rectangle, mark a dot ½″ from both the upper right and bottom left corners. On the wrong-side-up rectangle, mark a dot ½″ from the lower right and upper left corners.

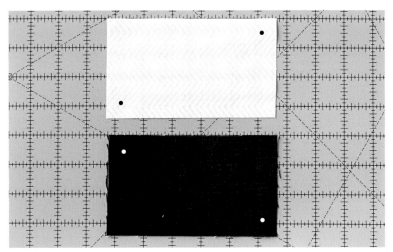

NW-pointing half-rectangle triangle dot placement

6. Mark each pair of NW-pointing rectangles in this same manner.

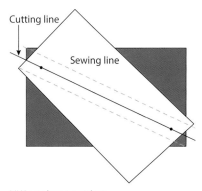

NW sewing + cutting

PIECING *the* BLOCKS

1. Sew ¼″ on either side of the marked lines. Check the first of both the NE- and NW-pointing rectangles to make sure everything is positioned correctly. Check again after sewing all the rectangles.

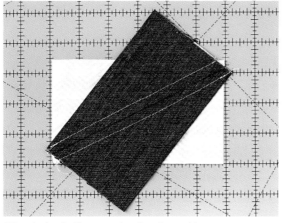

NE-pointing half-rectangle triangle marking

NW-pointing half-rectangle triangle marking

2. Cut each rectangle pair on the line between the 2 seams.

3. Press open and trim to 5½″ × 2¾″.

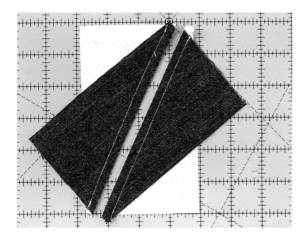

Tip: *Trimming Half-Rectangle Triangles*

To facilitate trimming half-rectangle triangles, use the HRT cutting pattern (pullout page P2) to make a cutting template. Align the diagonal line with the half-rectangle triangle seam and trim ¼″ to the outside of the template on all sides.

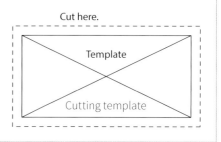

Cut here.

Template

Cutting template

APRON TOP ASSEMBLY

1. Place the blocks on a design wall to plan the apron top, using an improvised layout or following the apron assembly diagram (below).

2. Working in columns, sew together the half-rectangle triangle blocks and the remaining Fabric A rectangles. Press the seams open.

3. Sew together the columns, making sure to match intersecting seams as you sew. Press the seams open.

4. Press the apron top and trim the edges to approximately 30½″ × 26½″.

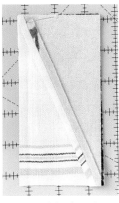

Tip: Perfect Points

Using a positioning pin is my favorite way to match intersecting seams. Traditionally, you insert a positioning pin into the layers at a 90° angle to perfectly align the seams, insert another pin to secure the placement, and remove the positioning pin. I typically sew with the position pin in until the last minute (and without inserting a second pin); I usually get a perfectly matched point.

Use a positioning pin for perfect points

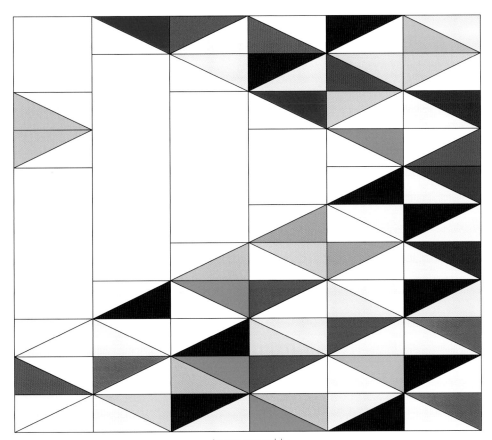

Apron assembly

Finishing

1. Make the apron ties by folding each apron-tie strip in half lengthwise, right sides together, and sewing a short end and the long edge at a ¼″ seam allowance. Using a loop turner or your favorite method, turn each tie right side out and press.

2. Cut the apron backing fabric the same size as the apron top, minus ³⁄₁₆″ from the width and length. This ensures that the backing does not show from the front of the apron.

3. Pin each tie with the raw end aligning with the top of the apron, ⅜″ down from the top and aligned with the sides of the apron, as shown.

4. Place the apron backing right sides together with the apron front, tucking the ties inside. **(A)**

5. Stitch together the sides. Turn right side out and press the side seams. The apron front should extend very slightly over the apron back.

6. Turn right sides together and sew the top and bottom, leaving approximately an 8″ opening on the bottom of the apron.

7. Turn right side out. Blindstitch or topstitch the bottom opening.

8. Press the apron, being sure the seams sit just to the underside of the apron. Baste together the layers and quilt as desired.

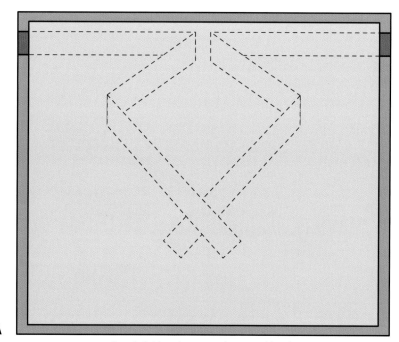

A

Sandwiching the apron front and back

Family Heritage Quilt
MITALI, MADHURI + LILA

Mitali is mother of three, writer, knitter, doctor, and expert sandwich maker. Born in New York and raised in Texas, she now lives in Montreal. Mitali's quilt was made from saris belonging to her maternal grandmother, Lila Chatterji.

Mitali and her daughters, Leena and Sonya

Photo from the Chatterji family's collection

Mitali's maternal grandparents

Remembering

My grandmother was born in British India, the oldest of three. She loved the arts, especially music, and she trained in the classical sitar.

One of my only clear memories of my grandmother is shelling sweet peas with her and thinking how small but flavorful the food was in India—the head of cauliflower, the chicken, the potatoes.

I'd like to talk to my grandmother about her story, hear about her life. All I'm left with are feelings of being hugged, fed, and loved.

On connection to the past

There are very few photographs, letters, or ephemera from that time in India. None of my great-grandmother, and very few of my grandmother—only the ones we took when we visited from Texas. The saris are the things she left behind.

There's this connection to my ancestors that goes beyond DNA, something spiritual and profound. I'd like my kids, who are mixed race, to remember their South Asian heritage. The cultural connection is becoming a fading echo. My grandmother left West Bengal for New Delhi. Then my mom left New Delhi for New York. I was born in New York, grew up in Texas, and now live in Canada. I speak better French than Bengali. I like Indian food and Bollywood movies but also enchiladas and country music.

There's this human longing for connection, not just to other people but also to ourselves, to our past, to our own stories. A quilt is a map of that. Like a mosaic, putting pieces together to tell a story not just about the past but about the present. Something new out of something old; something saved, something cherished.

About the clothing

To introduce another dimension of cultural context, we used saris from India. My mom has been storing them in a hard-shell blue American Tourister suitcase since she arrived in America.

They are really beautiful textiles, some woven with real gold and silver thread. Some of them belonged to my grandmother. They will serve as tactile memories, feelings, longings—a reminder.

MADHURI, MITALI'S MOM: The sari with a red border belonged to my grandmother. She wore it for praying. My mother used it for *puja*, and I wore it for my dad's funeral prayers. It has adorned three generations of women of our family; now it will be part of a quilt for my daughter and grandchildren. My mom must be smiling, because she wanted me to buy a new sari but I always wanted that one.

Saris used in the quilt

On DNA and generations

It's incredible to think that this 1 fabric was wrapped around 3 women, across 100 years, during times of ritual and reflection. Traces of oil from the skin, the residue of incense—the stories that are woven in that fabric!

Mitali, Madhuri + Lila: Mandala

Finished quilt: 45″ × 60″

Materials

Yardages are based on 40″ usable width, except where noted. Refer to Preparing Clothing for Quilting (page 22) to prepare the clothing fabric listed below before cutting it. Clothing quantities are approximate.

QUILTING COTTON: ⅛ yard of 4 fabrics in colors coordinating with clothing

CLOTHING/SENTIMENTAL FABRIC: 6–12 pieces of kid or adult clothes in 2 different color groups *or* 2 yards total of sentimental fabric

FABRIC A (UPPER BACKGROUND): 2¼ yards

FABRIC B (LOWER BACKGROUND): ⅞ yard *or* ⅞ yard of 2 fabrics for different corners

FABRIC C (LOWER CENTER BACKGROUND): 1 fat eighth of quilting cotton *or* 1 piece of clothing

BACKING: 3 yards

BATTING: 53″ × 68″

BINDING: ½ yard

QUILTING RULER WITH 45°-ANGLE MARK

TEMPLATE MATERIAL, such as Visi-GRID Quilter's Template Sheets (by C&T Publishing)

NONPERMANENT MARKING TOOL, such as a Hera Marker

Fabric: Best suited for fabric weights similar to quilting cotton.

Personalization: Quilt Design

To create a quilt for Mitali that represented her diverse cultural heritage, I combined a traditional Lone Star block and a Dresden-inspired medallion based on a mandala, representing her Texan and Indian roots, respectively. The Canadian and Québécois cultural element is represented by the overlapping triangles at the bottom of the quilt—one for each of the languages spoken in Canada.

Cutting

Using the petal piece patterns 1–5 (pullout page P2), trace and cut templates from template material. Note: For petal 3, tape two sheets of template material together to make the template. Transfer all markings and notches.

Measure twice + cut once!

LONE STAR BLOCK

From each quilting cotton, cut:

• 1 strip 1½″ × width of fabric

From clothing/sentimental fabric, cut:

• 4 strips 1½″ × 40″ in color group 1

• 1 strip 1½″ × 40″ in color group 2

MANDALA BLOCK

From clothing/sentimental fabric, cut:

• 32 rectangles 6″ × 1½″

• 4 squares 5¼″ × 5¼″. Subcut into 8 half-square triangles.

• 4 pieces each from the 5 petal templates, *template right side up*, in color group 2. Mark the notches as shown on the templates.

• 4 pieces each from the 5 petal templates, *template right side down*, in color group 2. Mark the notches as shown on the templates.

BACKGROUND

From Fabric A, cut:

• 1 rectangle 45″ × 34″

• 1 half-square triangle 32½″ × 32½″

From Fabric B, cut:

• 1 square 27½″ × 27½″. Subcut into 2 half-square triangles.

From Fabric C, cut:

• 1 half-square triangle 7″ × 7″

Piecing

Seam allowances are ¼″ unless otherwise noted. Refer to the quilt assembly diagram (page 126) as needed.

LONE STAR BLOCK SECTIONS

1. Combine the 9 quilting cotton & clothing 1½″ × 40″ strips to create 3 sets of 3 strips. Sew Strip Sets A, B, and C as shown, offsetting the ends of the rectangles by 1″. Press the seams to one side, the same direction in each strip.

A   B   C

2. Align the 45° angle of a quilting ruler with the top of Strip Set A, right side up, and trim the offset end. **(A)**

3. Measure 2½˝ from the trimmed edge and cut the first diamond strip. Cut 3 more diamond strips, each measuring 2½˝ from the last cut.

4. Flip the remainder of Strip Set A to be wrong side up. Align the 45° angle of the quilting ruler with the top of Strip A, right side up, and trim to create 4 diamond strips facing the opposite direction from those created in Step 3. **(B)**

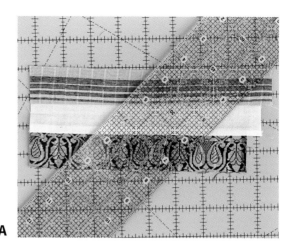

A

B

5. Repeat Steps 2–4 for Strip Sets B and C.

6. Sew together 1 each of diamond strips A, B, and C, following the layout as shown. Press the seams to one side. Repeat 3 more times with the other diamond strips of this orientation. The placement is the same for each group of 3.

7. Sew together the remaining 4 sets of diamond strips to create mirror-image diamond groups. **(C & D)**

C   D

ECHO SECTIONS

1. Sew 4 rectangles 6″ × 1½″ to a 5¼″ × 5¼″ half-square triangle, offsetting each rectangle by 1″, as shown. Align the 45° mark on the ruler along the bottom edge of the half-square triangle, and trim the offset ends on both sides of the rectangles. **(A)**

2. Sew 3 more half-square triangle Echo Sections with the offset in the same direction. Trim in the same manner as Step 1.

3. Sew and trim 4 half-square triangle Echo Sections, with the half-square triangle and rectangle offset facing the opposite direction. **(B)**

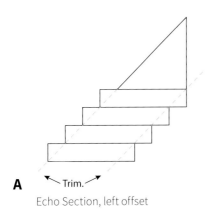

A

Echo Section, left offset

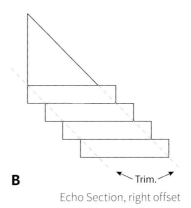

B

Echo Section, right offset

PETAL SECTIONS

1. Sew together 1 each of Petal Sections 1, 2, and 3, being careful to align the notches. Press the seams toward the outer edge. **(C)**

2. Repeat Step 1 for 3 sections facing the same direction and 4 sections facing the opposite direction.

3. Sew together 1 each of Petal Sections 4 and 5. Press the seams toward the outer edge. **(D)**

4. Repeat Step 3 for 3 sections facing the same direction and 4 sections facing the opposite direction.

5. Sew together 1 Petal Section 1/2/3 to Petal Section 4/5, as shown. Press the seams toward the outer edge. **(E)**

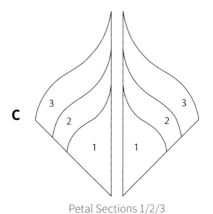

C

Petal Sections 1/2/3

D

Petal Sections 4/5

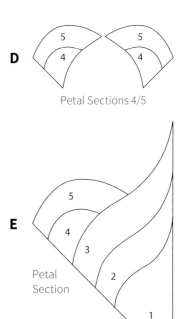

E

Petal Section

MANDALA SECTIONS

1. Sew the Lone Star block section to the half-square triangle Echo Section, as shown (below). Press the seams open.

2. Sew the Petal block section to the piece created in Step 1. Press the seams open. Repeat for the remaining 7 Mandala Sections. **(F)**

3. Sew together 2 Mandala Sections as shown, creating mirror images for the Petal Sections. **(G)**

4. Repeat Step 3 for the remaining 3 sections.

5. Sew together 2 of the mirrored sections. Press the seams open. Repeat with the other mirrored sections.

6. Sew together the 2 halves created in Step 5. Press the seam open.

7. Press the Mandala Block.

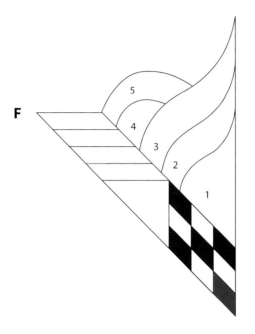

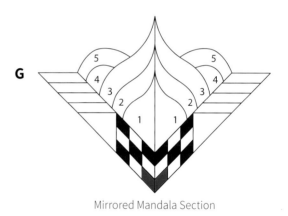

Mirrored Mandala Section

QUILT TOP ASSEMBLY

1. Aligning the 7″ × 7″ Fabric C half-square triangle with the 27½″ × 27½″ Fabric B half-square triangle as shown, use a nonpermanent marking tool to mark the edge of the 7″ × 7″ half-square triangle on the 27½″ × 27½″ half-square triangle. **(H)**

2. Remove the 7″ × 7″ triangle. Trim the 27½″ × 27½″ half-square triangle ½″ on the other side of the line (toward the closest point) marked in Step 1.

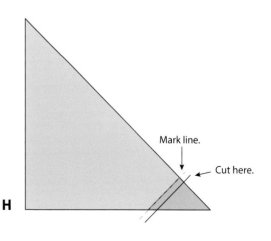

Mark line.

Cut here.

H

3. On the second 27½″ × 27½″ Fabric B half-square triangle, repeat Steps 1 and 2 on the left side.

4. Sew together the right trimmed 27½″ × 27½″ Fabric B half-square triangle from Step 2 and the 7″ × 7″ half-square triangle as shown in the background piecing diagram (below). Press the seams open.

5. Sew together the 32½″ × 32½″ Fabric A half-square triangle and the left trimmed 27½″ × 27½″ Fabric B half-square triangle as shown. Press the seams open.

6. Sew together the pieces created in Steps 4 and 5 as shown. Press the seams open.

Sew this to the 45″ × 34″ Fabric A rectangle. Press the seams open. **(I)**

7. Press and trim the quilt top background to 45½″ × 60½″.

8. Mark the center lengthwise on the quilt top. Position the mandala, using the centerline as a guide, and baste the mandala to the quilt top. **(J)**

9. Appliqué the mandala to the quilt top using a straight stitch, zigzag stitch, blanket stitch, or stitch of your choice. Press the quilt top.

I

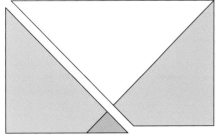

Background piecing

J

Quilt assembly

Finishing

Layer the quilt top, batting, and backing to make a quilt sandwich.
Baste, quilt, and bind using your preferred methods.

Family Quilt

LIZ, KARL, TRISTAN + LAYLA

Elizabeth, born in Guatemala, immigrated to Canada when she was seven. She is a doula and entrepreneur in Montreal, where she lives with her husband, Karl, and their children, Tristan and Layla.

On identity, loss, and rebirth

Being an immigrant was challenging. My mother struggled with the longing of returning home while simultaneously making a home in Victoria, British Columbia. When my mother died in 1996, everything that defined us died.

My quilt contains clothing or textiles that belong to or represent my family, as well as a *manta* that represents my family, country, and story.

About family, clothing with meaning, and defining moments

My Guatemalan weaving: After my mother died, I traveled to Guatemala alone. While visiting a weaver's coop, a young girl, who took a liking to me, made me a weaving. With Mayan symbols of strength, renewal, and rebirth, it represented my past and present. She said that even with all my sadness there was a lot to look forward to.

Karl's tie: Karl and I met in Vancouver, and on the last day of his 48-hour visit, we agreed we wanted to move forward in life together. Karl's tie is included because he loves to dress up. He wants to respect tradition, but there is always a unique element in what he wears.

Tristan's T-shirts: When Tristan was six, I returned from Guatemala with a shirt for him. He wore it for one week, and then said, "Mama, now I know that I am Guatemalan, too."

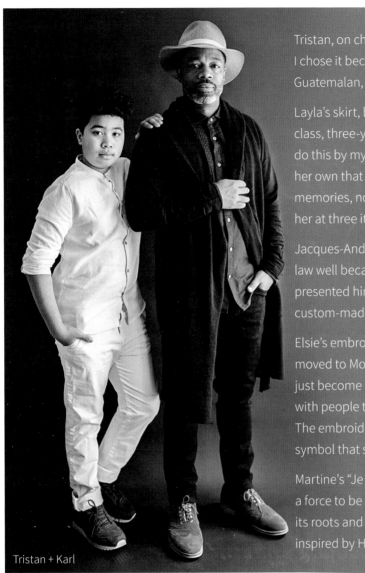

Tristan + Karl

Tristan, on choosing clothing for the quilt: I chose it because it's part of who I am—Haitian, Guatemalan, and born in Vancouver.

Layla's skirt, bodysuit, and dress: At her first ballet class, three-year-old Layla said, "Mama, I can do this by myself. You stay here." She came into her own that day. For clothes, Layla is attached to memories, not the physical pieces—I had to stop her at three items. She wanted to donate so many!

Jacques-André's blazer: I didn't know my father-in-law well because of a language barrier. The way he presented himself—always in his Sunday best, with custom-made jackets—was very important to him.

Elsie's embroidered napkins: When Karl and I moved to Montreal, we lived with his mother. I had just become a mom, left my home, and moved in with people that didn't know me or speak English. The embroidered napkins were a gift from Elsie: a symbol that she accepted me.

Martine's "Je Love Haiti" shirt: My sister-in-law is a force to be reckoned with—protector of family, its roots and history. She created a line of T-shirts inspired by Haiti after the earthquake in 2012.

On history, storytelling, and meaning

The quilt is our story brought to life. It represents the work we put in to make our family work, and each piece holds individual memories and represents our unique identities—who we are, where we're from, and how we "fit." It is a celebration of past and present, and excitement for the future.

Liz, Karl, Tristan + Layla: Mosaic

Finished size: 50¼″ × 50″

Materials

Yardages are based on 40″ usable width, except where noted. Refer to Preparing Clothing for Quilting (page 22) to prepare the clothing fabric listed below before cutting it. Clothing quantities are approximate.

KID OR ADULT CLOTHING IN DIFFERENT COLORS: 6–12 pieces

QUILTING COTTON IN COLORS COORDINATING WITH CLOTHING: 3–6 fat eighths or scraps

SENTIMENTAL FABRIC: 50¾″ × 17½″ piece *or* 1 yard of quilting cotton, pieced as desired

BACKING: 3¼ yards

BATTING: 58″ × 58″

BINDING: ½ yard

Fabric: Good for all. Thick fabric friendly.

Cutting

Measure twice + cut once!

BLOCK 1

From clothing or clothing/quilting cotton combination, cut:

Cut the following for each *block. You need 6 blocks total.*

- 1 rectangle 3″ × 8½″ (A)
- 1 rectangle 3″ × 5″ (A)
- 2 rectangles 4¾″ × 4½″ (B)
- 1 rectangle 4¾″ × 5″ (B)
- 1 rectangle 3¼″ × 4½″ (C)
- 1 rectangle 3¼″ × 5¼″ (C)
- 1 rectangle 3¼″ × 2¼″ (C)
- 1 rectangle 3¼″ × 2½″ (C)
- 1 rectangle 3½″ × 11″ (D)

- 1 rectangle 3½″ × 2½″ (D)
- 1 square 3½″ × 3½″ (Row 1)
- 1 rectangle 10″ × 3½″ (Row 1)

From quilting cotton, cut:

- 6 strips 13″ × 1½″ (horizontal)
- 6 strips 1½″ × 17″ (vertical)

BLOCK 2

From clothing or quilting cotton, cut:

- 1 rectangle 4½″ × 3½″ (Row 1)
- 1 rectangle 7″ × 3½″ (Row 1)
- 1 rectangle 6½″ × 3½″ (Row 1)
- 1 rectangle 17″ × 3½″ (Row 2)

BLOCK 3

From clothing or clothing/quilting cotton combination, cut:

Cut the following for each *block. You need 2 blocks total.*

- 2 rectangles 4¾″ × 4½″ (A)
- 1 rectangle 4¾″ × 5″ (A)
- 1 rectangle 3″ × 8½″ (B)
- 1 rectangle 3″ × 5″ (B)
- 1 strip 7¼″ × 1½″ (Row 1)
- 1 rectangle 7¼″ × 3½″ (Row 1)

Piecing

Seam allowances are ¼″ unless otherwise noted. Refer to the quilt assembly diagram (next page) as needed.

BLOCK 1

1. With right sides together, sew together the rectangles for Columns A, B, C, D, and Row 1 as shown in the Block 1 diagram. Press the seams open.

2. Sew together Columns A, B, C, and D as shown. Press the seams open.

3. Sew the 13½″ × 1½″ strip to the bottom of the columns pieced together in Step 2, and sew Row 1 to the bottom of the strip. Press the seams toward the dark side.

4. Sew the 1½″ × 17″ strip to the side of the block sewn together in Step 3. Press the seams toward the dark side.

5. Repeat Steps 1–4 for a total of 3 blocks 14″ × 17″. **(A)**

6. Repeat Steps 1–4, but use the Block 1 reverse diagram for placement to make 3 units of Block 1 reverse. **(B)**

Design Tip

To add more depth to the quilt, try using the same color placement in each block but varying the value.

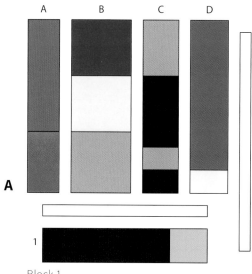

Block 1

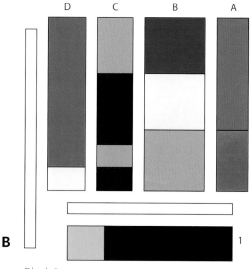

Block 1 reverse

BLOCK 2

1. Sew together the 3 smaller rectangles as shown. Press the seams open.

2. Sew the 17″ rectangle to the bottom of the strip sewn in Step 1. Press the seams open. The block should measure 17″ × 6½″. **(C)**

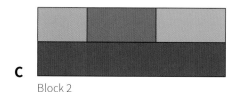

Block 2

BLOCK 3

1. Sew together the rectangles for Columns A and B and Row 1 as shown. Press the seams open.

2. Sew together Columns A and B, and sew Row 1 to the bottom as shown. Press the seams open.

3. Repeat Steps 1 and 2 for the second block. The blocks should measure 7¼″ × 17″. **(D)**

Block 3

QUILT TOP ASSEMBLY

1. Arrange the blocks as shown. Sew together the blocks into columns, as shown; then sew the columns together. Press the seams open.

2. Sew the block created in Step 1 to the top of the 50¾″ × 17½″ rectangle. Press the seams open.

3. Square and trim the quilt top to 50¾″ × 50½″. **(E)**

Finishing

Layer the quilt top, batting, and backing to make a quilt sandwich. Baste, quilt, and bind using your preferred methods.

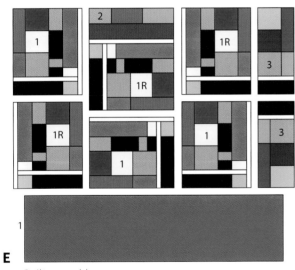

E

Quilt assembly

Papa and Son Quilt

MICHEL + LUCA

The last quilt brings us back to the beginning: Michel's quilt is the first modern heirloom memory quilt I made. It was the quilt that launched a new passion and new business for me. But more importantly, it was a place to put my overflowing love for Michel and our then three-year-old son, Luca. Michel had his first heart transplant at the age of 30 and now awaits a second transplant—we are all too aware of how things can change in an instant.

As much as I wanted to preserve our son's babyhood in a quilt and to remember all of those milestones and happy memories, I also wanted to create something to comfort Michel—something to celebrate his relationship with Luca, now nine, and remind him of the unbreakable bond between father and son.

Photos by Vivian Doan

About Luca

MICHEL: Luca is my son, my one and only child. Luca is intelligent, kind, and empathic. He is a very quiet boy, attractive and singular looking, but he doesn't want to be singled out. He's his own person and likes to be around people but doesn't necessarily need to be a part of the group. What I admire most about Luca is that he is, by nature, kind.

About Michel

LUCA: Papa is special to me because he's my dad. I love that he's funny and makes jokes. We like to watch movies together. I wish I was very tall like him. Papa's love makes me feel happy and safe.

On favorite memories

MICHEL: They've all been really favorite memories. A few years ago we went to New Brunswick, and he just dropped trou and played in the water. He was just happy and didn't care what anyone else thought.

On what the perfect day together looks like

MICHEL: We go out to enjoy the outdoors. We discover something new. He teaches me something and vice versa.

LUCA: Papa and I would be at La Ronde [amusement park] together. And we would become millionaires. And ride roller coasters. We would eat duck confit and steak, with chocolate ice cream for dessert.

Photos by Suzanne Paquette

Luca's clothing on the back of Michel's quilt

On having the quilt made with their clothing, and the importance of preserving memories

MICHEL: I love having something made by hand with care, something that a lot of time and effort was put into, something that I use every day. And the quilt is the perfect weight for summer.

LUCA: If I know how to, I will make a quilt for my future kids [if I have them]. I would tell them that my mom made one and that I wanted to try to make one. If someone dies, you can go to your room and remember all the good things that happened.

I like knowing that my clothes are in the quilt. It's a good souvenir to have a quilt made with my clothes and Papa's clothes.

Michel + Luca: Modern Arrow

Finished quilt: 72″ × 90″

Materials

Yardages are based on 40″ usable width, except where noted. Refer to Preparing Clothing for Quilting (page 22) to prepare the clothing fabric listed below before cutting it. Clothing quantities are approximate.

FABRIC A (BACKGROUND/OFF-WHITE): 5 yards of quilting cotton

FABRIC B (BEIGE): Approximately 1–2 pieces of adult clothing or 6–12 pieces of baby/kid clothing *or* 1 yard of quilting cotton

FABRIC C (DARK BEIGE): Approximately 1 piece of adult clothing or 3–10 pieces of baby/kid clothing *or* ⅓ yard of quilting cotton

FABRIC D (GRAY): Approximately 1–2 pieces of adult clothing or 8–12 pieces of baby/kid clothing *or* ⅔ yard of quilting cotton

FABRIC E (DARK TURQUOISE): Approximately 1 piece of clothing *or* quilting-cotton scraps

FABRIC F (LIGHT TURQUOISE): Approximately 1 piece of clothing *or* quilting-cotton scraps

FABRIC G (BLACK): ⅜ yard of quilting cotton

FABRIC H (VARIOUS): Approximately 8–11 pieces of clothing *or* quilting-cotton scraps in various colors

FABRIC SCRAPS IN 2 DIFFERENT COLORS for arrow appliqué

FUSIBLE WEBBING: 3″ × 16″

BACKING: 6¾ yards

BATTING: 80″ × 98″

BINDING: ¾ yard

TEMPLATE MATERIAL, such as Visi-GRID Quilter's Template Sheets (by C&T Publishing)

Fabric: Good for most.

Quilt Design Inspiration

The design of Michel & Luca's quilt was inspired by *Meistermappe des Staatlichen Bauhauses* (1923) by Bauhaus painter and photographer László Moholy-Nagy.

In addition to loving the clean lines and symbiotic relationship to quilting, I love that its design roots are in *constructivism*—an artistic and architectural philosophy that originated in Russia in 1913—very appropriate for Michel, who has a degree in Russian studies.

Tip: Transparency Effect

If you would like to achieve the transparency effect as shown, be mindful of the fabrics or clothing you pick for Fabrics B, C, and D. They should each be light, mid, and dark tones of a similar color.

MICHEL + LUCA: MODERN ARROW

Cutting

Using the arrow base pattern (pullout page P2), trace and cut a template from template material. Transfer all markings.

Measure twice + cut once!

FROM FABRIC A, CUT:

- 1 strip 10½″ × 90½″ (A)
- 1 strip 6½″ × 70½″ (B1)
- 2 rectangles 6½″ × 10½″ (B3, G5)
- 1 strip 4″ × 60″ (C1)
- 2 squares 4″ × 4″ (C3, D5)
- 1 strip 4″ × 90″. Subcut into 3 strips 4″ × 26½″ (D1, E1, F1).
- 4 rectangles 4″ × 10½″ (C5, D7, E8, F7)
- 1 strip 6½″ × 50½″ (G1)
- 1 rectangle 18½″ × 50½″ (J1)
- 1 rectangle 18½″ × 10½″ (J5)
- 1 strip 4″ × 50½″ (K1)
- 1 rectangle 4″ × 17″ (K3)
- 1 strip 9½″ × 90½″ (L)
- 1 rectangle 4″ × 6½″ (H24)

For the parallelogram piecing, cut:

- 2 squares 2⅞″ × 2⅞″. Subcut into 4 half-square triangles (I1, I19, I23, I25).
- 1 rectangle 2½″ × 3¼″ (I1)
- 1 rectangle 2½″ × 4¼″ (I19)
- 1 rectangle 2½″ × 5¼″ (I23)
- 1 rectangle 2½″ × 1½″ (I25)
- 1 strip 2½″ wide × 40″. Subcut into 8 parallelograms with the following heights:
  3 parallelograms 4½″ high (I7, I11, I17)
  1 parallelogram 2¾″ high (I9)
  4 parallelograms 3¾″ high (I3, I5, I13, I15)

Tip: Small Clothing?

If the clothing is not big enough for the larger pieces, sew a few pieces of clothing together as desired.

FROM FABRIC B, CUT:

- 1 strip 4″ × 34″ (D2)
- 2 strips 4″ × 24½″ (E2, F2)
- 1 rectangle 18½″ × 7″ (J4)
- 1 rectangle 6½″ × 10½″ (B2)
- 1 rectangle 6½″ × 7″ (G4)
- 2 rectangles 4″ × 10½″ (C4, D6)
- 2 rectangles 4″ × 7″ (E7, F6)
- 1 rectangle 2½″ × 7″ (I24)

FROM FABRIC C, CUT:

- 1 rectangle 4″ × 14″ (F3)
- 1 rectangle 4″ × 10″ (E3)
- 2 squares 4″ × 4″ (E6, F5)
- 1 rectangle 6½″ × 4″ (G3)
- 1 rectangle 2½″ × 4″ (I21)
- 1 rectangle 4″ × 18½″ (J3)
- 10 parallelograms, each 2½″ wide, with the following heights:
  2 parallelograms 2″ high (I6, I16)
  1 parallelogram 2¼″ high (I10)
- 5 parallelograms 2¾″ high (I2, I4, I12, I14, I24)
- 2 parallelograms 3″ high (I8, I18)

FROM FABRIC D, CUT:

- 1 square 4″ × 4″ (E5)
- 1 rectangle 4″ × 7½″ (F4)
- 1 rectangle 6½″ × 20½″ (G2)
- 1 rectangle 2½″ × 20½″ (I20)
- 1 rectangle 18½″ × 20½″ (J2)
- 1 rectangle 4″ × 24″ (K2)

FROM *BOTH* FABRICS E + F, CUT:

- 1 rectangle 4″ × 7½″ (C2, E4)
- 1 square 4″ × 4″ (D3, D4)

FROM FABRIC G, CUT:

- 11 parallelograms 4″ wide with
  the following heights:

  4 parallelograms 4¼″ high (H7, H11, H17, H21)

  6 parallelograms 2½″ high (H3, H5, H9, H13, H15, H19)

- 1 rectangle 4″ × 12½″ (H23)

- 1 half-square triangle 4⅜″ × 4⅜″ (H23)

- 1 square 2⅜″ × 2⅜″ (Fold the square in half and cut on the diagonal to create the triangle arrowhead appliqué.)

- 1 rectangle ⅝″ × 14⅜″ (arrow appliqué)

- 1 arrow base pattern (arrow appliqué)

FROM FABRIC H, CUT:

- 10 parallelograms 4″ wide with
  the following heights:

  4 parallelograms 4¼″ high (H8, H10, H18, H20)

  1 parallelogram 5¼″ high (H22)

  1 parallelogram 17″ high (H12)

  4 parallelograms 2½″ high (H4, H6, H14, H16)

- 1 parallelogram 1½″ high (H2)

- 1 rectangle 4″ × 5⅝″. (Place the rectangle horizontally on the cutting mat and trim the right side to a 45° NW angle for H1.)

FROM THE ASSORTED SCRAPS FOR THE ARROW APPLIQUÉ AND THE FUSIBLE WEB, CUT:

Note: *Measurements do not include seam allowance.*

- 1 rectangle ⅜″ × 14⅜″ (arrow shaft)

- 10 parallelograms 1″ wide with
  the following heights:

  6 parallelograms 1⅛″ high

  4 parallelograms ⅜″ high

Piecing

Seam allowances are ¼″ unless otherwise noted. Refer to the quilt assembly diagram (page 140) as needed.

QUILT TOP

1. With right sides together and working from top to bottom, sew together the pieces of each column with ¼″ seams, following the column order in the quilt assembly diagram (page 140). Use the Columns H + I cutting and piecing diagram (at right) for those columns. Press all seams open after constructing each column.

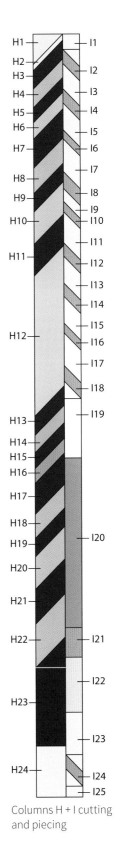

Columns H + I cutting and piecing

2. Working from left to right, pin and sew together Columns B–K, making sure to match aligning pieces together. Press the seams open.

3. Pin and sew the 2 outer strips (A and L) to the left and right sides of the quilt top. Press the seams open.

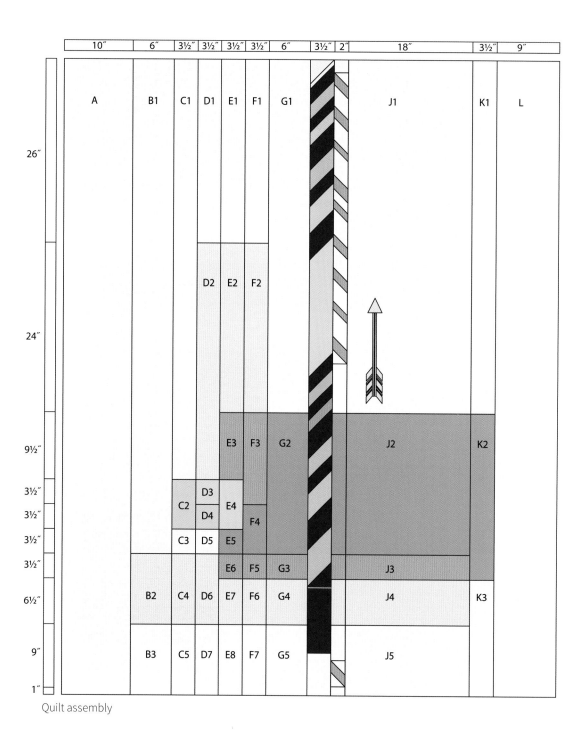

Quilt assembly

Finishing

Layer the quilt top, batting, and backing to make a quilt sandwich. Baste, quilt, and bind using your preferred methods.

APPLIQUÉ

Preparing

1. Position the arrow parallelogram and shaft pieces on top of the base piece. The fusible web should align perfectly with, and be hidden by, the top arrow pieces.

2. With a dry iron, fuse together the arrow layers.

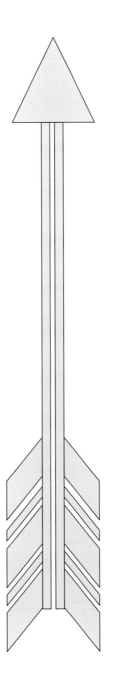

Sewing

1. Position the arrow on the quilt top. Hand baste it into place.

2. Machine or hand embroider around the arrow edges.

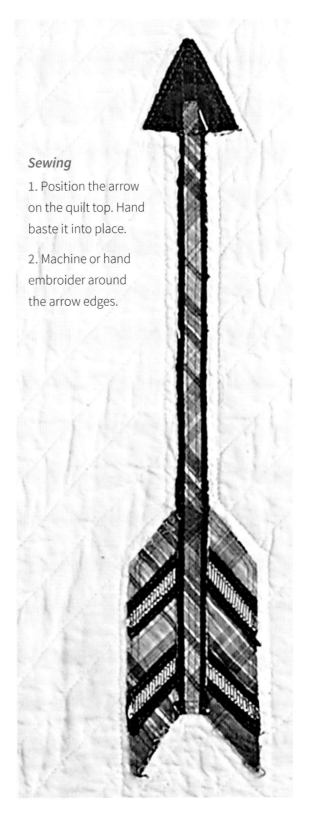

MODERN MEMORY QUILTS

About the Author

SUZANNE PAQUETTE is a modern quilter, designer, and creative director. Through her company, Atelier Six, Suzanne designs quilt patterns and creates modern heirloom memory quilts, combining her love of modern aesthetics and the emotional engagement of objects with meaning. Her work has appeared in many books (*Modern Quilts*, *Handmade Getaway*, and *The T-Shirt Quilt Book*) and quilt exhibitions (QuiltCon 2017 and 2018, and Montreal Modern Quilt Guild's exhibition: *Moderniser la Courtepointe*, 2016). When she's not creating for Atelier Six, Suzanne works with the team at Camelot Fabrics as their marketing director.

Suzanne's design education and experience have taken twists and turns, all eventually leading to modern memory quilting. After graduating with a bachelor of applied arts in fashion design from Ryerson University and working in costume for Broadway shows, she launched her millinery line and retail store, Six Degrees, on Queen West in Toronto—her first foray into the entrepreneurial world. In 2001, Suzanne ran away with the circus to work with *Cirque du Soleil* for 12 years as creative lead in consumer product development for over 25 international shows. It was at *Cirque* that the spark of bringing emotional depth to creative work was ignited and where she learned that "*impossible* is only a word."

Suzanne's work has appeared in *The New York Times*, *Toronto Star*, *Montreal Gazette*, *Elle Québec*, *We Seek* (e180), and other publications. She lives in Montreal with her family, including Daisy the dog and Squirrel the cat.

Visit Suzanne online and follow on social media!

WEBSITE: ateliersixdesign.com
(Be sure to check out her blog!)

FACEBOOK: /ateliersixdesign

PINTEREST: /the_milliner

INSTAGRAM: @the_milliner

Want even more creative content?

Make it, snap it, share it *using* *#ctpublishing*